Puggles

The Owner's Guide from Puppy to Old Age

Choosing, Caring for, Grooming, Health, Training and Understanding Your Puggle Dog or Puppy

By Morgan Andrews

Copyright and Trademarks

This publication is Copyright © 2015 by CWP Publishing.

ISBN: 978-1-910677-03-2

A catalogue record for this book is available from the British library.

Disclaimer and Legal Notice

This product is not legal or accounting advice and should not be interpreted in that manner. You need to do your own due-diligence to determine if the content of this product is right for you. While every attempt has been made to verify the information shared in this publication, neither the author nor the affiliates assume any responsibility for errors, omissions or contrary interpretation of the subject matter herein. Any perceived slights to any specific person(s) or organization(s) are purely unintentional.

We have no control over the nature, content and availability of the web sites listed in this book. The inclusion of any web site links does not necessarily imply a recommendation or endorse the views expressed within them. CWP Publishing takes no responsibility for, and will not be liable for, the websites being temporarily unavailable or being removed from the internet.

The accuracy and completeness of information provided herein and opinions stated herein are not guaranteed or warranted to produce any particular results, and the advice and strategies contained herein may not be suitable for every individual. The author shall not be liable for any loss incurred as a consequence of the use and application, directly or indirectly, of any information presented in this work. This publication is designed to provide information in regard to the subject matter covered.

Neither the author nor the publisher assume any responsibility for any errors or omissions, nor do they represent or warrant that the ideas, information, actions, plans, suggestions contained in this book are in all cases accurate. It is the reader's responsibility to find advice before putting anything written in this book into practice. The information in this book is not intended to serve as legal advice.

Foreword

Although I have known both Pugs and Beagles personally, the first time I saw a Puggle — the product of pairing a male Pug with a female Beagle — I had no real idea what I was seeing beyond a really cute, energetic, medium-sized dog. I struck up a conversation with the owner in a vet clinic waiting room and received an invitation to visit her kennel.

We formed a friendship and I came to know several of her dogs quite well. I can assure you, there are few forces of nature equal to a litter of Puggle puppies! When they plant their paws and let out with a burst of Pug-like barking that ends in a proper hound howl, they are absolutely adorable.

Puggles are ranked as one of the top three most popular hybrid companion breeds in America. They are intelligent, affectionate dogs that live happily in small spaces, including apartments, with only minimal exercise needs. With a lifespan of 15 years and few health problems, the breed is attractive to singles and families alike.

Although somewhat given to chasing cats, Puggles typically get along well with other dogs and are excellent with children. They are sturdy little dogs who love to run and run and then run some more! They can keep up with even the most energetic toddler. Often kid and dog collapse into the same heap, with even more cuteness ensuing.

For all their positive points, Puggles can be incredibly stubborn, and if they have not been properly crate trained, can suffer from separation anxiety. This reaction can include the full gamut of bad behaviors: barking, howling, chewing, and digging. The dogs also must be kept leashed while on walks. They are scent dogs and will take off after a "trail" while completely ignoring your attempts to call them back.

Factor in a fair amount of shedding, especially as the warm months are coming on, and a reputation for being slow to housebreak, and it's clear that Puggles are not without their challenges. But to be fair, what breed isn't?

If you are looking for a small to medium-sized dog with an excellent personality that will live happily in any space and has low exercise needs, the Puggle could be the perfect companion.

Many of the world's top breeders have been involved in contributing to this book, and once you've read it, you will have all the information you need to make a well-informed decision about whether the Puggle is the breed for you.

As an owner, expert trainer and professional dog whisperer, I would like to teach you the human side of the equation, so you can learn how to think more like your dog and eliminate behavioral problems with your pet.

The information in this book will help you to form a fuller sense of what life with a Puggle would be like and arm you with the correct questions to ask in your discussions with breeders. No pet purchase should be undertaken without careful consideration. This is particularly true for a breed as special, and at times enigmatic, as the Puggle.

Acknowledgments

In writing this book, I also sought tips, advice, photos and opinions from many experts of the Puggle breed.

In particular, I wish to thank the following wonderful experts for going out of their way to help and contribute:

AUSTRALIA

Lauren Goodman of Cottage Canines
http://www.cottagecanines.com/

USA & CANADA

Doug Edmiston of Pugglesville
http://www.pugglesville.com/

John & Margie Couch of Hugapuggle
http://www.hugapuggle.com/

Jeanine and Brad Ross of PuggleBaby.com
http://www.pugglebaby.com

Jason & Jennifer Yates of Rainbowland Puggles
http://www.rainbowlandpuggles.com

Danielle Schnell of LuvAPuggle.com
http://www.luvapuggle.com/

Doreen Mcleod of Breezy Hill Farm
http://www.breezy-hills.com/

Kindra Mazurek of Colorado Puggles
http://www.coloradopuggles.com

UNITED KINGDOM

Mo DeVille of PuggleUK
http://www.puggleuk.co.uk/

PHOTOGRAPHY

Rebecca Youngbar (Owner of Murlin)
Trevor Bowling (Photographer of Samson)
Tony Kamenicky (Owner of Layla)
Carol VanHook (Owner of Smokey)
Ashley Edward Steinbach (Photographer of Lexie, owner Adrienne Steinbach)
Joerg Schubert (Owner of Parker)
Mike & Tiffany Werner (Owners of Dexie & Morgan)
Lynn Smart (Owner of Bramble)

Table of Contents

Table of Contents

Table of Contents

Table of Contents

Table of Contents

Table of Contents

Chapter 1 – Meet the Puggle

A "Puggle" is a hybrid dog created by breeding a male Pug and a female Beagle. Genetically, most Puggles available today are F1 dogs born from such a crossing. Female Pugs are not big enough to carry the larger puppies. Most attempts at hybridization with female Pugs end in the death of the offspring and the mother.

Photo Credit: Murlin from Rebecca Youngbar

As the popularity of the Puggle breed continues to grow, more people are breeding Puggles to Puggles to refine the genetic mix and to standardize the breed. When that happens, it will be possible to more accurately predict Puggle appearance and temperament.

Like all first generation hybrid breeds, the Puggle's personality can go one of two ways. When the genetic mix is perfect, the Puggle is a healthy, robust and playful dog that exhibits the Pug's trademark sense of humor. Under less ideal circumstances, the Beagle's determination meets the Pug's stubbornness head on, and you get an uncooperative dog that won't listen to a word you say.

These are the chances that all hybrid dog owners take, but Puggles at their best are excellent, well-rounded companions. They will live happily in apartments, get along brilliantly with other pets and children, and are affectionate and loving. Not to mention the fact that they're just too cute for words!

What Is the Difference Between F1, F1b and F2?

Since the breed is still relatively "new," it is quite common for available puppies to be first generation (F1) crosses between a Pug and a Beagle.

If an F1 Puggle is bred to another F1 Puggle, the puppies would be classified as F2s.

Jeanine and Brad Ross of PuggleBaby.com explain: "A first generation Puggle is a cross between a purebred Pug and a purebred Beagle – there are unscrupulous breeders out there that cross with other breeds and call them 'Puggles.' There should be NO BRINDLE-colored Puggles, because brindle is not a color ever seen genetically in Pugs or Beagles.

There are also 2nd generation Puggles, which is either breeding a Puggle to Puggle or F1B, which is breeding a Puggle back to either a Pug or a Beagle. Most F1B breedings are done by breeding back to a Pug, and the Puggles that are then 3/4 Pug, look VERY Puggish, and just have a slight snout.

Puggles are a very hearty and healthy mix, the biggest problem that we ever have is Cherry Eye, which happens in maybe 1% or less."

Puggle Breed History

The practice of intentionally allowing two dogs of different breeds to produce offspring, known as crossbreeding (hybridization), is hardly new, but purists have typically frowned upon it. In recent years, however, crossbreeding has grown in popularity out of a desire to create breeds that more accurately match the changing role of dogs in our lives.

The modern pampered pooch is not the working animal of years past, nor is he a creature that lives outdoors most of his life. Dogs have firmly claimed their role as beloved family companions – in fact as members of the family – and breeders, in response, have altered their goals. Many popular crossbreed mixes are cultivated specifically for their excellent natures and for their ability not just to live, but also to thrive in a domestic setting.

In the 1980s, a dog fancier in Wisconsin, Wallace Havens, developed the first Puggles and subsequently registered the breed with the American Canine Hybrid Club. Although still not recognized by the American Kennel Club or The Kennel Club in the United Kingdom, the Puggle is now widely regarded as a distinct and popular breed in its own right.

(The dogs can also be registered with the International Designer Canine Registry. There are local and regional Puggle clubs in the United States and Great Britain, but no overall governing bodies for the breed at this time.)

Dedicated Puggle breeders are working hard to improve the genetics of the hybridization so that the dogs breed true, reliably passing on their best characteristics to the next generation.

Although some hybridizations are nothing more than poorly considered "designer dogs," the Puggle mix is an excellent combination of two hardy breeds and will undoubtedly gain independent recognition by the various canine governing organizations in the years to come.

At this juncture of the Puggle's evolution, it's useful to understand a little bit about the two foundation breeds to gain more insight into what you can expect of your hybrid pet.

Photo Credit: Murlin from Rebecca Youngbar

Pug Breed History

The Pug breed is believed to have developed in China. The first Pugs were imported to Europe from China in the 16th century, and the breed served as the official dog of the House of Orange. For this reason, they have sometimes been called the Dutch Mastiff. In 1688, when William III and Mary II left the Netherlands to accept the British throne, a Pug went with them. In time, the dogs became popular throughout Europe.

The breed's somewhat fanciful appearance led them to be used in interesting ways. In Italy, for instance, Pugs were employed as carriage dogs, dressed in clothing to match the coachman's uniform! While thought of today as a toy companion or "lap" breed, Pugs have done their fair share of work. The dogs have been used by the military as trackers, and they are also excellent watch dogs.

Pugs appeared in the artwork of William Hogarth, including his self-portrait dating from 1745 that hangs in the Tate Gallery in London. In the 19th century, Queen Victoria kept many Pugs, even breeding the dogs. Her Majesty's enthusiasm for dogs in general helped to support the establishment of the Kennel Club in 1873, which remains the governing canine body in the United Kingdom today.

Many of the Pugs that appear in paintings from the 18th and 19th century had longer legs and faces than the modern breed, which likely began to emerge after 1860. This evolution was helped by an infusion of new blood from dogs imported directly from China. These animals had the modern Pug look, with short legs and a flat nose.

The Pug arrived in the United States in the 19th century, where the dogs immediately became favored as both show dogs and family pets. The American Kennel Club recognized the breed in 1885, but the Pug Dog Club of America was not founded until 1981.

Beagle Breed History

Like many breeds, the exact origins of the Beagle are uncertain. As early as the 5th century BCE, however, hunting dogs of a similar description were being used in Greece. In the 8th century, the St. Hubert Hound, a scent dog, was used to create the Talbot Hound, a breed brought to England by William the Conqueror in the 11th century. To improve the dogs' running abilities, they were crossed with greyhounds.

Those dogs are believed to be the ancestor of the Beagle, a name first used for very small creatures that stood just 8-9 inches / 20.32-22.86 cm tall. This miniature breed, sometimes called the Pocket Beagle, went extinct in 1901. In the 18th century, two breeds, the Southern Hound and the North Country Beagle, were crossed with larger breeds to create the Foxhound, and in the 1840s, the standard Beagle.

By 1887, there were 18 packs of Beagles in England. The breed was imported to the United States in the early 1870s. The American Kennel Club recognized the Beagle in 1884, and the breed rapidly came to be prized for both its hunting abilities and its quality as a family dog.

The name "Beagle" derives from the French "begueule," meaning "open throat," and the Gaelic "beag" for small. If you've ever heard a Beagle throw back its head and bay, there's no question the name is an apt one.

Puggle Breed Characteristics

But what do you get when you mix the two breeds? Puggles are small to medium-size dogs. Their faces are loaded with expressive character because they have both the wrinkled, wizened look of the Pug and the large, luminous Beagle eyes and long, floppy Beagle ears.

Although the snout is shorter than a Beagle's, it is not as "smooshed" as that of a Pug. Some enthusiasts say the resulting look is vaguely Buddha-like. The tail is held high over the back like a Pug's, but the degree of curl varies, and the length is closer to that of the Beagle.

Puggles tend to be active, intelligent dogs that require at least two 15-minute walks per day. Because they have a scent hound heritage, they like to "pick up the trail" and follow it, so keeping them leashed during outings is essential.

Like Pugs, however, Puggles are funny and fun loving. They make exceptional family dogs because they are affectionate and interested in everything that's going on around them. Pugs like to be smack in the middle of things, and Puggles are pretty much true to that side of their ancestry.

The breed's coat is low maintenance, although their ears and eyes do have to be cleaned regularly. Puggles do quite well across all types of living environments, including apartments, and are highly adaptable. If untrained, however, they can be quite stubborn and given to problem barking. Again, that's the hound in them.

One advantage of all hybrid breeds is that they tend to be much healthier than either parent breed. Puggles have a more elongated snout, which eliminates the breathing problems that are associated with the Pug. Although in theory a Puggle can be susceptible to any condition or illness present in either parent breed, this mix has proven to be quite sturdy and has a projected lifespan of up to 15 years or more.

It should be noted that because Puggles are companion animals, they do want to be with their humans. The breed can suffer from separation anxiety, which is a powerful trigger for other negative behaviors including barking, howling, chewing, and digging.

We asked breeder Kindra Mazurek of Colorado Puggles why she thinks Puggles are so special: "Puggles are special because they have the very best characteristics of both the Pug and Beagle. They get along well with other animals and children."

Physical Size

Size varies widely, but all Puggles fall in a range of 18-30 lbs. / 8.16-13.6 kg and stand 8-15 inches / 20.32-38.1 cm at the shoulder. This varies depending on the size of the Beagle used for the cross. For example, Doreen Mcleod of Breezy Hill Farm says: "I refer to my Puggles as 'PeeWee' Puggles. They are much smaller than standard Puggles because I cross a smaller Beagle, a registered 'Olde English Pocket Beagle' with my small AKC Pugs to get a smaller Puggle that averages 12" tall and weighs in the 10-13 lb. range."

Photo Credit: Doreen Mcleod of Breezy Hill Farm

Coat and Color

The Puggle's double coat is short and smooth with a dense undercoat and a slightly longer topcoat. This makes for relatively low maintenance responsibilities for the owner, but the dogs do shed and should be brushed weekly. They shed twice a year – once in the spring and then again in the fall.

Colors include fawn, red, tan, lemon, and black. Mixed colors are rare, although particolor dogs with white on their bodies do occur. Fawn is the most common coat, typically with the Pug's trademark black mask.

Personality and Temperament

With hybrid dogs, it's more difficult to make hard and fast predictions on personality and temperament. Given proper training with lots of patience and consistent rewards for correct behaviors, Puggles are friendly, affectionate, comical, and get along well with strangers.

Since temperament is an inherited characteristic, your best bet in meeting a litter of puppies is to look for the dog that is not overly bossy or shy. With a dog that is more or less in the middle, you can mold his friendly nature in the first four months with solid socialization. That is the time when puppies are most receptive to new sights, places, people, sounds, and experiences — like doggie kindergarten.

The Puggle Puppy

Bringing a new puppy home is fun, even if the memories you're making include epic, puppy-generated messes! Young dogs are a huge responsibility no matter how much you love them, and they take a lot of work. Puggle puppies can be assertive and aggressive if they're not properly trained.

The first few weeks with any dog is an important phase that shapes the animal's adult behavior and temperament. Every new pet owner hopes to have a well-mannered, obedient, and happy companion.

With young Puggles, you'll be faced with curbing incessant barking, chewing, digging, and ankle biting. They have boundless energy, a lot of willpower, and the manipulative ability only a preciously cute little dog can muster.

Pugs are notoriously hard to housebreak, rarely figuring out where to "go" before six months of age. This may or may not be the case with your Puggle puppy, but plan for the worst-case scenario and factor this into your consideration of the pros and cons of the breed.

Also, be prepared for moderate to heavy shedding and for the required "facials." Puggles, like Pugs, have wrinkles and creases where fungal infections can develop without regular cleaning.

With Other Animals

Puggles have an excellent reputation with other animals, but like most dogs, they do have a tendency to chase cats, which is not a good way to facilitate détente with Fluffy. If the cat stays still, there isn't anything to chase. They will run after anything that moves quickly – even a piece of litter blowing in the wind!

Never force the animals to interact or to spend time together. When the Puggle puppy first arrives, put the little dog in its crate and allow other pets in the house to check out the new family member on their own terms and at their own speed. Carefully observe the reactions on both sides of the meeting and take your cues from how it's all going.

Supervise all interactions. Reinforce good behavior with treats and praise. At the first sign of aggression or "trash talking," separate the animals with a firm "no" and try again later. Understand this can go on for several weeks until your pets reach some form of agreement whose terms only they will comprehend.

Photo Credit: John & Margie Couch of Hugapuggle

Puggles and Children

The Puggle does very well when raised with kids, but I don't think it is a good idea to have ANY dog with children under 3-4 years old. Prior to that, they don't understand pinching, pulling, and grabbing is not OK, and the dog could bite in self-defense. Wait until your children are 4-5 years of age, when they are old enough to understand the Puggle disposition and to respect his boundaries.

Pugs and Beagles both have high energy levels that make them good dogs for children. They are active but not "hyper." Pugs actually seem to love children, and this trait comes through in the Puggle mix.

The dogs like exercise and have an entertaining, fun sense of humor that lends itself to game play. Plus, from the Beagle side of the family, Puggles get a special love for running full out.

Regardless of any breed's reputation for good nature, I always tell parents that they must spend the necessary time to teach their children how to interact kindly with all kinds of animals. If a child hurts any dog by pulling its ears or tail or even biting the creature, the dog can hardly be blamed for reacting, but you'll find that a Puggle will put up with quite a lot and maintain his perfect humor.

Which Is Better – Male or Female?

Typically, my position on gender is that it doesn't matter. Concentrate instead on the personality of the individual dog. This line of thinking seems to hold true for Puggles, with no discernible difference in the temperament of females over males.

Don't fall for the idea that female dogs are sweeter. It's a groundless assumption, and one that is often wrong, especially with intact individuals experiencing hormonal shifts. Most experts agree that females that have been spoiled and coddled when young show more territoriality than adult males.

The greatest negative behaviors cited for male dogs of any breed are spraying and territorial urine marking. In the case of purebred adoptions, having the animal spayed or neutered is a condition of the purchase agreement.

Breeders make pet-quality animals available because they do not conform to the accepted breed standard. Such dogs are not suitable for exhibition or for use in a breeding program. Spaying and neutering under these circumstances protects the integrity of the breeder's bloodlines.

Regardless, "best practice" advocates altering an animal before 6 months of age. Reduced hormone levels stop spraying in males and moodiness when a female is in heat, but the procedures do nothing to alter the dog's core personality. The real determining factor in any dog's long-term behavior is the quality of its treatment and training.

Puppy or Adult Dog?

People love puppies for all the obvious reasons. They are adorable, and the younger the dog is at adoption, the more time you will have with your pet. At an average lifespan prediction of as much as 15 years, longevity shouldn't be a "deal breaker" if you do find an adult dog in need of adoption.

Any time you welcome a shelter dog into your home, it is imperative that you understand the circumstances under which the animal was surrendered. Puggles are rarely given up for aggression, but problem behaviors could be at the root of their homelessness.

Puggles can be incessant barkers and, if untrained, can have destructive tendencies to chew and dig. Because they are such good dogs in small living conditions, however, it is not uncommon to see a Puggle surrendered to a rescue group simply because its human owner can no longer care for a pet due to old age or illness.

I am a huge advocate of all animal rescue organizations. The numbers of homeless companion animals in need of adoption stands at shocking levels. To give one of these creatures a "forever" home is an enormous act of kindness. You will be saving a life.

Puggles are wonderful dogs. If your heart is set on one, I understand why. But if you are searching for a loyal four-legged friend of any breed, please do not rule out a shelter adoption.

Regardless of the breed you choose, please support rescue organizations. Such groups are always in need of donations and volunteer hours. When you do adopt a rescue dog, find out as much as possible about the dog's background.

One or Two?

When you're confronted with an adorable litter of Puggle puppies, your heart may tell you to go ahead and get two. Listen to your brain! Owning one dog is a serious commitment of time and money, but with two dogs, everything doubles: food, housebreaking, training, vet bills, boarding fees, and time.

I would recommend pacing yourself and starting with just one Puggle. The breed is tolerant and welcoming of new additions to the family, so adding a second Puggle in the future won't be a problem if one is not enough for you.

Breeder Mo DeVille of PuggleUK says: "Puggles do like company. Puppies that have gone from here have had, variously, cats, rabbits, and even a chipmunk as companions as well as other breeds of dog. They are happier with a canine companion, and pairs of Puggles will exercise each other as they will happily play together for hours. I wouldn't recommend two puppies at the same time though – a 12 month gap is advisable."

The Need for Socialization

Any breed, no matter how well regarded for its temperament, can still develop bad habits and become obnoxious. Puggle puppies are stubborn. They also have some hound-like tendencies inherited from their Beagle genetics, including barking and downright howling. All of these things absolutely can be addressed and controlled with training, but your dog's education must start no later than 10-12 weeks of age.

(Finish the rabies, distemper, and parvovirus vaccinations before exposing the puppy to other dogs.)

During formal training, understand you will be in "school" as much as your Puggle. If you don't want to be putty in his paws, do your homework and listen to the trainer!
Your job is to be the "alpha," a responsibility for which many humans are ill equipped without some in-class time of their own!

Breeder Mo DeVille of PuggleUK advises: "The most important thing to understand when training your puppy is that it needs rules and routine. Never confuse it by your actions. If, for instance, the puppy isn't going to be allowed to sit on the furniture, don't ever sit with it on your lap. It doesn't understand the difference between being on your lap on a chair and just being on the chair without your lap! If it isn't allowed on the furniture but you want it on your lap, go down to its level and sit on the floor with it. If you break any of the rules of the routine just once, you will be in for a bumpy ride!"

Famous Puggles and Their Owners

As Puggles become more popular, their cute good looks and outstanding nature will undoubtedly win them a place with the rich and famous. Some celebrities who have already embraced the breed include:

- Uma Thurman
- Jake Gyllenhaal
- Sly Stallone
- Julianne Moore

Chapter 2 - The Puggle Breed Standard

A breed standard is created to codify all the best traits of a breed to provide a basis by which exceptional examples of the dog may be judged in competition and for breeding purposes. Since the Puggle is not an official breed, the following are the standards for the Pug and the Beagle. This will give you some idea of the traits and look of the Puggle based on the two foundation breeds.

The American Kennel Club (AKC) standards are produced verbatim. The only changes incorporated are typographical to enhance readability.

AKC Official Standard for the Pug

General Appearance:

Symmetry and general appearance are decidedly square and cobby. A lean, leggy Pug and a dog with short legs and a long body are equally objectionable.

Size, Proportion, Substance:

The Pug should be multum in parvo, and this condensation (if the word may be used) is shown by compactness of form, well-knit proportions, and hardness of developed muscle. Weight from 14 to 18 pounds (dog or bitch) desirable. Proportion square.

Head:

The head is large, massive, round – not apple-headed, with no indentation of the skull. The eyes are dark in color, very large, bold and prominent, globular in shape, soft and solicitous in expression, very lustrous, and, when excited, full of fire. The ears are thin, small, soft, like black velvet. There are two kinds – the "rose" and the "button." Preference is given to the latter. The wrinkles are large and deep. The muzzle is short, blunt, square, but not upfaced. Bite – A Pug's bite should be very slightly undershot.

Neck, Topline, Body:

The neck is slightly arched. It is strong, thick, and with enough length to carry the head proudly. The short back is level from the withers to the high tail set. The body is short and cobby, wide in chest and well ribbed up. The tail is curled as tightly as possible over the hip. The double curl is perfection.

Forequarters:

The legs are very strong, straight, of moderate length, and are set well under. The elbows should be directly under the withers when viewed from the side. The shoulders are moderately laid back. The pasterns are strong, neither steep nor down. The feet are neither so long as the foot of the hare, nor so round as that of the cat; well split-up toes, and the nails black. Dewclaws are generally removed.

Hindquarters:

The strong, powerful hindquarters have moderate bend of stifle and short hocks perpendicular to the ground. The legs are parallel when viewed from behind. The hindquarters are in balance with the forequarters. The thighs and buttocks are full and muscular. Feet as in front.

Coat:

Fine, smooth, soft, short and glossy, neither hard nor woolly.

Color:

The colors are fawn or black. The fawn color should be decided so as to make the contrast complete between the color and the trace and mask.

Markings:

The markings are clearly defined. The muzzle or mask, ears, moles on cheeks, thumb mark or diamond on forehead, and the back trace should be as black as possible. The mask should be black. The more intense and well defined it is, the better. The trace is a black line extending from the occiput to the tail.

Gait:

Viewed from the front, the forelegs should be carried well forward, showing no weakness in the pasterns, the paws landing squarely with the central toes straight ahead. The rear action should be strong and free through hocks and stifles, with no twisting or turning in or out at the joints. The hind legs should follow in line with the front. There is a slight natural convergence of the limbs both fore and aft. A slight roll of the hindquarters typifies the gait, which should be free, self-assured, and jaunty.

Temperament:

This is an even-tempered breed, exhibiting stability, playfulness, great charm, dignity, and an outgoing, loving disposition.

Disqualification:

Any color other than fawn or black.

AKC Official Standard for the Beagle

Head:

The skull should be fairly long, slightly domed at occiput, with cranium broad and full.

Ears – Ears set on moderately low, long, reaching when drawn out nearly, if not quite, to the end of the nose; fine in texture, fairly broad – with almost entire absence of erectile power-setting close to the head, with the forward edge slightly inturning to the cheek; rounded at tip.

Eyes – Eyes large, set well apart; soft and houndlike-expression gentle and pleading; of a brown or hazel color.

Muzzle – Muzzle of medium length; straight and square-cut; the stop moderately defined.

Jaws – Level. Lips free from flews; nostrils large and open.

Defects – A very flat skull, narrow across the top; excess of dome, eyes small, sharp and terrier-like, or prominent and protruding; muzzle long, snipy or cut away decidedly below the eyes, or very short. Roman-nosed, or upturned, giving a dish-face expression. Ears short, set on high or with a tendency to rise above the point of origin.

Body:

Neck and Throat – Neck rising free and light from the shoulders; strong in substance yet not loaded, of medium length. The throat clean and free from folds of skin; a slight wrinkle below the angle of the jaw, however, may be allowable.

Defects – A thick, short, cloddy neck carried on a line with the top of the shoulders. Throat showing dewlap and folds of skin to a degree termed "throatiness."

Shoulders and Chest:

Shoulders sloping; clean, muscular, not heavy or loaded– conveying the idea of freedom of action with activity and strength. Chest deep and broad, but not broad enough to interfere with the free play of the shoulders.

Defects – Straight, upright shoulders. Chest disproportionately wide or with lack of depth.

Back, Loin and Ribs:

Back short, muscular and strong. Loin broad and slightly arched, and the ribs well sprung, giving abundance of lung room.

Defects – Very long or swayed or roached back. Flat, narrow loin. Flat ribs.

Forelegs and Feet:

Forelegs – Straight, with plenty of bone in proportion to size of the hound. Pasterns short and straight.

Feet – Close, round and firm. Pad full and hard.

Defects – Out at elbows. Knees knuckled over forward, or bent backward. Forelegs crooked or Dachshund-like. Feet long, open or spreading.

Hips, Thighs, Hind Legs and Feet:

Hips and thighs strong and well-muscled, giving abundance of propelling power. Stifles strong and well let down. Hocks firm, symmetrical and moderately bent. Feet close and firm.

Defects – Cowhocks, or straight hocks. Lack of muscle and propelling power. Open feet.

Tail:

Set moderately high; carried gaily, but not turned forward over the back; with slight curve; short as compared with size of the hound; with brush.

Defects – A long tail. Teapot curve or inclined forward from the root. Rat tail with absence of brush.

Coat:

A close, hard, hound coat of medium length.

Defects – A short, thin coat, or of a soft quality.

Color:

Any true hound color.

General Appearance:

A miniature Foxhound, solid and big for his inches, with the wear-and-tear look of the hound that can last in the chase and follow his quarry to the death.

Varieties:

There shall be two varieties: Thirteen Inch – which shall be for hounds not exceeding 13 inches in height. Fifteen Inch – which shall be for hounds over 13 but not exceeding 15 inches in height.

Disqualification: Any hound measuring more than 15 inches shall be disqualified.

Chapter 3 – Getting Serious About Adoption

When you have moved past the stage of just "window shopping" for a dog and think you're pretty well settled on a Puggle, there are questions you need to ask yourself and some basic education you should acquire.

Photo Credit: Doug Edmiston of Pugglesville

Is a Puggle the Dog for You?

There's a degree of certainty that comes with a pedigreed adoption that is absent with a hybrid dog. I was raised with dogs we called "mutts," that were the product of random crossbreeding. There is nothing random about crossbreeding Pugs and Beagles.

Both are well-established breeds with a complementary set of physical and emotional traits. You have a very good chance of knowing exactly what you will get in a Puggle, so long as you acquire your pet from a breeder dedicated to developing and promoting this emerging breed.

If, however, you get your Puggle from a "backyard" breeder, or worse yet, fall prey to a puppy mill operation, there is no guarantee about the animal's genetic background. Most dogs born into such circumstances are, frankly, a genetic mess and can suffer all kinds of physical and behavioral problems.

The kinds of questions you want to ask yourself before you adopt a Puggle should explore both the positives and the potential negatives of the adoption.

- Do you understand that your dog's Pug blood may make the Puggle difficult to housebreak and that the process can take as long as six months?

- Can your life accommodate the physical and emotional needs of a small but highly energetic breed with known issues regarding separation anxiety?

- If your dog does develop separation anxiety, are you prepared to find appropriate ways to deal with the potential problem behaviors like barking, howling, chewing, and digging that may result?

- Will you commit to brushing your dog weekly and to cleaning its facial folds and wrinkles daily if needed?

You will not have the same level of consistency in choice that is the hallmark of purebred dogs purchased from breeders with carefully crafted bloodlines, but unlike many hybrid crosses, there is a fairly standard Puggle "look."

Your main choices will be "male or female" and "puppy or adult." While some people feel that simplifies things greatly, there are specific considerations relative to both of these choices.

Do You Need a License?

Before you bring your Puggle home, you need to think about whether there are any licensing restrictions in your area. Some countries have strict licensing requirements for the keeping of particular animals.

Even if you are not legally required to have a license for your Puggle, you might still want to consider getting one. Having a license for your dog means that there is an official record of your ownership so, should someone find your dog when he gets lost, that person will be able to find your contact information and reconnect you with him.

There are no federal regulations in the United States regarding the licensing of dogs, but most states do require that dogs be licensed by their owners, otherwise you may be subject to a fine.

Fortunately, dog licenses are inexpensive and fairly easy to obtain – you simply file an application with the state and then renew the license each year. In most cases, licensing a dog costs no more than $25.

Finding and Picking a Puppy

Typically, the first step in finding a specific type of puppy is tracking down a reputable breeder. This can be harder with a hybrid breed. Thankfully, in the case of the Puggle, the mix is getting more common, and there are many excellent breeders in the United States and Great Britain.

Before the "Aw Factor" kicks in and you are completely swept away by the cuteness of a Puggle puppy, familiarize yourself with basic quick health checks you can make even as you are playing with a young dog up for adoption.

- Although a puppy may be sleepy at first, the dog should wake up quickly and be both alert and energetic.

- The little Puggle should feel well fed in your hands, with some fat over the rib area.

- The coat should be shiny and healthy with no dandruff, bald patches, or greasiness.

- The baby should walk and run easily and energetically, with no physical difficulty or impairment.

- The eyes should be bright and clear, with no sign of discharge or crustiness.

- Breathing should be quiet, with no excessive sneezing or coughing and no discharge or crust on the nostrils.

- Examine the area around the genitals to ensure there is no visible fecal collection or accumulation of pus.

- Test the Puggle's hearing by clapping your hands when the baby is looking away from you and judge the puppy's reaction.

- Test vision by rolling a ball toward the Puggle, making sure the puppy appropriately notices and interacts with the object.

When you have educated yourself about what to look for in a healthy puppy, move on to visiting breeder websites or speaking over the phone to owners in whose dogs you are interested. You want to arrive at a short list of potential breeders from which to pick. Plan to visit more than one such facility before making your decision.

Locating Breeders to Consider

At this stage of the Puggle's establishment as a breed, most people looking for one are forced to search for breeder websites online. I will discuss evaluating breeders more fully in the chapter on buying a Puggle.

For now, know that your best option is to obtain a dog from a breeder that is clearly serious about their breeding program and displays this fact with copious information about their dogs, including lots and lots of pictures.

Finding advertisements for Puggles in local newspapers or similar publications is dicey at best. You may simply be dealing with a "backyard breeder," a well-meaning person who has allowed the mating of two dogs of similar type.

There is nothing inherently wrong with this situation, although I do strongly recommend that an independent veterinarian evaluate the puppy before you agree to adopt it. All too often, however, if you go through the classified ads you can stumble into a puppy mill where dogs are being raised in deplorable conditions for profit only.

Never adopt any dog unless you can meet the parents and siblings and see for yourself the surroundings in which the dog was born and is being raised. If you are faced with having to travel to pick up your dog, it's a huge advantage to see recorded video footage, or to do a live videoconference with the breeder and the puppies.

It is far, far preferable to work with an owner from whom you can verify the health of the parents and discuss the potential for any congenital illnesses.

Responsible owners are more than willing to give you all this information and more, and are actively interested in making sure their dogs go to good homes. If you don't get this "vibe" from someone seeking to sell you a dog, something is wrong.

Photo Credit: Joerg Schubert owner of Parker

We asked owner Joerg Schubert what made him choose to buy a Puggle instead of another breed: "My wife saw a Puggle, not knowing what it was and thought like 'oh, that must be a cross-breed of a Pug and something else.' So we did some research and learned what a Puggle is. We found it cuter than a Pug and figured that hybrids in general tend to be healthier than pedigrees. So we found Parker and instantly fell in love with him."

The Timing of Your Adoption Matters

Be highly suspicious of any breeder that assures you they have dogs available at all times. It is normal, and a sign that you are working with a reputable operation, for your name to be placed on a waiting list.

(You may also be asked to place a small deposit to guarantee that you can adopt a puppy from a coming litter. Should you choose not to take one of the dogs, this money is generally refunded, but find out the terms of such a transaction in advance.)

Typically, females can only conceive twice a year, so spring or early summer is the best time to find a puppy. Breeders like to schedule litters for the warm months, so they can train their young dogs outside. Think about what's going on in your own life. Don't adopt a dog at a time when you have a huge commitment at work or there's a lot of disruption around an impending holiday.

Dogs, especially very smart ones like Puggles, thrive on routine. You want adequate time to bond with your pet and to help the little dog understand how his new world "runs."

Pros and Cons of Owning a Puggle

Talking about pros and cons for any breed always draws me up a little short. It's a very subjective business since what one person may love in a breed another person will not like at all.

I think Jack Russell Terriers are fantastically smart dogs, but they are also the drill sergeants of the canine world. I don't have any desire to give my life over to a dog that will run it at that level. My preference is for more laid-back breeds that value quiet companionship as highly as a rousing game of fetch.

People who love Puggles should be ready to talk about their good qualities as well as the challenges they pose for one overriding reason – a desire to see these very special animals go to the best home possible where they will be loved and appreciated.

Pros of Puggle Ownership

- Sociable. Get along well with other pets, children, and visitors.
- Like to play and spend time with their owners.
- Bond quickly and like to be cuddled.
- Intelligent and trainable, but stubborn.
- Minimal exercise needs.
- Adapt well to apartment living.

Cons of Puggle Ownership

- Get along well with other pets, but may chase cats.
- Stubborn. Start training before four months of age.
- Can be difficult to housebreak, which is a known Pug issue.
- Prone to separation anxiety and may bark, howl, chew, and dig.
- A shedding breed.
- Facial wrinkles and creases require cleaning.

It is imperative that new owners understand the potential for medical problems with any breed. The chapter on health includes a full discussion of such potential conditions.

We asked owner Rebecca Youngbar what made her buy her Puggle: "I bought a Puggle because they are advertised as a good dog for an apartment, and rather high energy. I wanted to have a walking companion and Murlin walked 3 miles a day with me very willingly."

Approximate Purchase Price

Prices vary widely. Puggle puppies for sale from reputable breeders cost approximately $500 / £772. Most breeders do not list prices on their home pages. You must contact them to discuss an adoption and the attendant costs.

Owner Tony Kamenicky says, "We paid $98 for Layla; she was abandoned at the local Humane Society."

We asked Mike & Tiffany Werner (Owners of Dexie & Morgan) if they were glad they bought a Puggle and not another breed: "Our answer to that question is yes! We initially chose the Puggle breed due their size and the fact that they look like forever puppies. After having our Puggle for three years, we truly knew that it was perfect breed for us, so much so that we added a second one."

These websites can be good places to begin your search:

Adopt a Pet — http://www.adoptapet.com
Petango — http://www.petango.com
Puppy Find — http://www.puppyfind.com/
Oodle - http://dogs.oodle.com/

Chapter 4 – Buying a Puggle

When you buy a pedigreed dog, you go through a detailed adoption process. You will almost certainly be required to spay or neuter the dog before it reaches six months of age in order to take possession of the registration papers.

When adopting a hybrid dog, however, you may be looking at almost any kind of "deal" absent or inclusive of the typical health guarantees, genetic information, medical records, and other details of a pedigree adoption arrangement.

How to Choose the Best Breeder

I don't advocate shipping live animals. Find a local breeder or one in reasonable traveling distance. Even if you find a breeder online, visit the facility at least once before adopting. Plan to pick the animal up in person.

Be suspicious of any breeder unwilling to allow such a visit or one that doesn't want to show you around the operation. You don't want to interact with just one puppy. You should meet the parent(s) and the entire litter.

It's important to get a sense of how the dogs live and their level of care. When you talk to the breeder owner, information should flow in both directions. The owner should discuss both the positives and negatives associated with the dogs.

What to Expect From a Good Breeder

Responsible breeders help you select a puppy. They place the long-term welfare of the dog front and center. The owner should show interest in your life and ask questions about your schedule, family, and other pets.

This is not nosiness. Breeders are Puggle experts. They should try to judge the correctness of the placement. Breeder owners who aren't interested in what kind of home the dog will have are suspect.

Nowadays, many breeders are home-based and their dogs live in the house as pets. Puppies are typically raised in the breeder's home as well. It's very common for Puggle breeders to use guardian homes for their breeding dogs. A guardian home is a permanent family for the dog. The breeder retains ownership of the dog during the years the dog is used for breeding, however, the dog lives with the guardian family. This arrangement is great for the dog because once retired from breeding, he/she is spayed/neutered and returned to its forever family. There is no need to re-home the dog after its breeding career has ended. There are still breeders who use kennels, but the numbers of home breeders is quite high.

The Breeder Should Provide the Following

Because Puggles are not an officially sanctioned breed, you may be dealing with a less formal adoption process. However, in the best of all possible worlds, the breeder will treat the arrangements as if the dog you are adopting is pedigreed and will provide the following items to you:

- The *contract of sale* details both parties' responsibilities. It also explains the transfer of paperwork and records.

- The *information packet* offers feeding, training, and exercise advice. It also recommends standard procedures like worming and vaccinations.

- The *description of ancestry* includes the names and types of Pug and Beagle used in breeding.

- *Health records* detail medical procedures, include vaccination records, and disclose potential genetic issues.

The breeder should **guarantee the puppy's health** at the time of adoption. You will be required to confirm this fact with a vet within a set period of time.

Warning Signs of a Bad Breeder

Always be alert to key warning signs like:

- Breeders that tell you it is not necessary for you to visit the facility in person.

- Assertions that you can buy a puppy sight unseen with confidence.

- Breeder owners that will allow you to come to their home or facility, but who will not show you where the dogs actually live.

- Dogs kept in overcrowded conditions where the animals seem nervous and apprehensive.

- Situations in which you are not allowed to meet at least one of the puppies' parents.

- Sellers who can't produce health information or that say they will provide the records later.

- No health guarantee and no discussion of what happens if the puppy does fall ill, including a potential refund.

- Refusal to provide a signed bill of sale or vague promises to forward one later.

Avoiding Scam Puppy Sales

No one wants to support a puppy mill. Such operations exist for profit only. They crank out the greatest number of litters possible, with an eye toward nothing but the bottom line.

The care the dogs receive ranges from deplorable to non-existent. Inbreeding is standard, leading to genetic abnormalities, wide-ranging health problems, and short lifespans.

The Internet is, unfortunately, a ripe advertising ground for puppy mills, as are pet shops. If you can't afford to buy from a reputable breeder, consider a shelter or rescue adoption. Even if you can't be 100% certain you're getting a bona fide Puggle, you are adopting an animal in need.

Puppy mills see profit, but give no thought to breeding integrity. Again, if you can't:

- visit the facility where the puppies were born

- meet the parents

- inspect the facilities

- and receive some genetic and health information

...something is wrong.

Best Age to Purchase a Puggle Puppy

A Puggle puppy needs time to learn important life skills from the mother dog, including eating solid food and grooming themselves.

For the first month of a puppy's life, they will be on a mother's milk-only diet. Once the puppy's teeth begin to appear, they will start to be weaned from mother's milk, and by the age of 8 weeks should be completely weaned and eating just puppy food.

Puppies generally leave between 10-12 weeks and are usually weaned before they receive their first vaccines. It is not beneficial for the pup to stay longer, as it can have a negative affect for several reasons. One is that the puppy should not have access to nursing after their first vaccine, otherwise that vaccine is void. Some moms will continue to nurse despite the puppy being on solid food.

In other cases, the mom is too overwhelmed with the size of the pups and the size of the litter and she avoids them. This occurs as early as 6 weeks old, and it can result in bad behaviors as the puppies interact with each other. Their roughhouse playing becomes more and more imprinted on them, and families could struggle to teach the puppy not to play with children as they do with their littermates.

Trainers would even highly recommend training and bonding begin with their new families by 8-10 weeks. In addition, pups need to be highly socialized between 8-12 weeks with new people, new experiences, and new places. This period is very crucial in developing a well-rounded pup.

Photo Credit: Kindra Mazurek of Colorado Puggles

How to Choose a Puppy?

My best advice is to go with the puppy that is drawn to you. My standard strategy in selecting a pup has always been to sit a little apart from a litter and let one of the dogs come to me. My late father was, in his own way, a "dog whisperer." He taught me this trick for picking puppies and it's never let me down.

I've had dogs in my life since childhood and enjoyed a special connection with them all. I will say that often the dog that comes to me isn't the one I might have chosen — but I still consistently rely on this method.

You will want to choose a puppy with a friendly, easy-going temperament, and your breeder should be able to help you with your selection. Also ask the breeder about the temperament and personalities of the puppy's parents and if they have socialized the puppies.

Always be certain to ask if a Puggle puppy you are interested in has displayed any signs of aggression or fear, because if this is happening at such an early age, you may experience behavioral troubles as the puppy becomes older.

Beyond this, I suggest that you interact with your dog with a clear understanding that each one is an individual with unique traits. It is not so much a matter of learning about all Puggles, but rather of learning about YOUR Puggle dog.

Checking Puppy Social Skills

When choosing a puppy out of a litter, look for one that is friendly and outgoing, rather than one who is overly aggressive or fearful. Puppies who demonstrate good social skills with their littermates are much more likely to develop into easy-going, happy adult dogs that play well with others. Observe all the puppies together and take notice:

Which puppies are comfortable both on top and on the bottom when play fighting and wrestling with their littermates, and which puppies seem to only like being on top?

Which puppies try to keep the toys away from the other puppies, and which puppies share?

Which puppies seem to like the company of their littermates, and which ones seem to be loners?

Puppies that ease up or stop rough play when another puppy yelps or cries are more likely to respond appropriately when they play too roughly as adults.

Is the puppy sociable with humans? If they will not come to you, or display fear toward strangers, this could develop into a problem later in their life.

Is the puppy relaxed about being handled? If they are not, they may become difficult with adults and children during daily interactions, grooming or visits to the veterinarian's office.

Photo Credit: Mike & Tiffany Werner owners of Dexie & Morgan

Chapter 5 – Caring for Your New Puppy

All puppies are forces of nature, and Puggles are no exception. The first four months of any dog's life is a critical period for training and socialization. In a dog like the Puggle, with a strong need to be a companion, this is the time when your new pet must learn to be crated while you are away to prevent separation anxiety.

Puggles get many hound traits from the Beagle side of their heritage. This can include problem barking and howling. It's cute in a tiny puppy, but disastrous in a grown dog. Never encourage your Puggle to howl by howling with him!

Photo Credit: Tony Kamenicky owner of Layla

A bored Puggle will also chew and dig. These traits make puppy proofing your home all the more important. Normal chewing, on appropriate toys, is a healthy activity for any dog. Your job is to put a stop to destructive chewing before it becomes a life habit.

Pugs are notoriously difficult to housebreak, which can also be an issue with Puggles. Expect the process to take at least six months. Crate training is also critically important for successful housebreaking lessons.

Like Pugs, Puggles also can become skilled beggars and are susceptible to weight gain. Put your foot down from the start and do not allow your dog to develop a fondness for human foods that will not only make him fat, but are also a health hazard in other ways.

Puggles can live as long as 15 years. Don't let any bad habits get started when your dog is a puppy, or you could be dealing with the consequences for years!

The Fundamentals of Puppy Proofing

Think of a Puggle puppy as a bright toddler with four legs. Get yourself in the mindset that you're bringing a baby genius home, and try to think like a puppy. Every nook and cranny invites exploration. Every discovery can then be potentially chewed, swallowed – or both!

Household Poisons

A dog, especially a young one, will eat pretty much anything, often gulping something down with no forethought.

Take a complete inventory of the areas to which your Puggle will have access. Remove all lurking poisonous dangers from cabinets and shelves. Get everything up and out of the dog's reach. Pay special attention to:

- cleaning products
- insecticides

- mothballs
- fertilizers
- antifreeze

If you are not sure about any item, assume it's poisonous and remove it.

Look Through Your Puggle's Eyes

Get down on the floor and have a look around from puppy level. Your new furry Einstein will spot anything that catches your attention and many things that don't!

Do not leave any dangling electrical cords, drapery pulls, or even loose scraps of wallpaper. Look for forgotten items that have been wedged behind cushions or kicked under the furniture. Don't let anything stay out that could be a choking hazard.

Tie up anything that might create a "topple" danger. A coaxial cable may look boring to you, but in the mouth of a determined little dog, it could send a heavy television set crashing down. Cord minders and electrical ties are your friends!

Remove stuffed items and pillows, and cover the legs of prized pieces of furniture against chewing. Take anything out of the room that even looks like it *might* be a toy. Think I'm kidding? Go online and do a Google image search for "dog chewed cell phone" and shudder at what you will see.

Plant Dangers, Inside and Out

The list of indoor and outdoor plants that are a toxic risk to dogs is long and includes many surprises. You may know that apricot and peach pits are poisonous to canines, but what about spinach and tomato vines?

The American Society for the Prevention of Cruelty to Animals has created a large reference list of plants for dog owners available at:

http://www.aspca.org/pet-care/animal-poison-control/toxic-and-non-toxic-plants

Go through the list and remove any plants from your home that might make your puppy sick. Don't just assume that your dog will leave such items alone.

Preparing for the Homecoming

Before you bring your new Puggle home, buy an appropriate travel crate and a wire crate for home use. Since the home crate will also be an important tool in housebreaking, the size of the unit is important.

Many pet owners want to get a crate large enough for the puppy to "grow into" in the interest of saving money. When you are housebreaking a dog, you are working with the principle that the animal will not soil its own "den." If you buy a huge crate for a small dog, the puppy is likely to pick a corner as the "bathroom," thus setting back his training.

Crates are rated by the size of the dog in pounds / kilograms. For example:

- For Puggles weighing up to 10 lbs. / 4.53 kg , the crate should be 19" x 12" x 15" / 48.26 cm x 30.48 cm x 38.1 cm.

Due to the difficulty of housebreaking this breed, resign yourself to having to buy a small crate for your puppy and then upgrading to a larger unit as your pet grows.

At a maximum adult size of 30 lbs. / 13.6 kg, your Puggle will ultimately require a crate that measures:

- 30″ x 19″ x 22″ / 76.2 cm x 48.26 cm x 55.88 cm

Put one or two puppy safe chew toys in the crate for the ride home along with a recently worn article of clothing. You want the dog to learn your scent. Be sure to fasten the seat belt over the crate.

Photo Credit: Mo DeVille of PuggleUK

Talk to the breeder to ensure the dog has not eaten. Take the puppy out to do its business before putting it in the crate. There may be whining and crying, but don't give in! Leave the dog in the crate! It's far safer for the puppy to ride there than to be in someone's lap.

Ideally, take someone with you to sit next to the crate and comfort the puppy.

Don't overload the dog's senses with too many people. No matter how excited the kids may be at the prospect of a new puppy, leave the children back at the house. The trip home needs to be calm and quiet.

As soon as you arrive home, take the puppy to a patch of grass outside to relieve himself. Immediately begin encouraging him for doing so. Positive and consistent praise is an important part of housebreaking.

Stick with the usual feeding schedule, and use the same kind of food the dog has been receiving.

Create a designated "puppy safe" area in the house. Give the puppy his privacy and let him explore on his own. Don't isolate the little dog, but don't crowd him either.

Give the Puggle soft pieces of worn clothing to further familiarize him with your scent. Leave a radio playing at a low volume for "company." At night, you may opt to give the baby a well-wrapped warm water bottle, but put the dog in its crate and do not bring it to bed with you.

I realize that last bit may sound all but impossible, but if you want a crate-trained dog, you have to start from day one. It's much, much harder to get a dog used to sleeping overnight in his crate after any time in the bed with you.

The Importance of the Crate

The crate plays an important role in your dog's life. Don't think of its use as "imprisoning" your Puggle. The dog sees the crate as a den and will retreat to it for safety, security, and privacy. Dogs often go to their crates just to enjoy quiet time.

When you accustom your dog to a crate as a puppy, you get ahead of issues of separation anxiety and prepare your pet to do well with travel. The crate also plays an important role in housebreaking, a topic we will discuss shortly.

Never rush crate training. Don't lose your temper or show frustration. The dog must go into the crate on its own. Begin by leaving the door open. Tie it in place so it does not slam shut on accident. Give your puppy a treat each time he goes inside. Reinforce his good behavior with verbal praise. Never use the crate as punishment. Proper use of the crate gives both you and your Puggle peace of mind.

Go Slow With the Children

If you have children, talk to them before the puppy arrives. Puggles are good dogs for children, but this will be the little dog's first time away from its mother, siblings, and familiar surroundings. The initial transition is important. Supervise all interactions for everyone's safety and comfort.

Help children understand how to handle the puppy and to carry it safely. Limit playtime until everyone gets to know each other. It will be no time before your Puggle and your kids are running around all over the house and yard — and Puggles love to run!

We asked John & Margie Couch of breeder Hugapuggle whether they think Puggles are suitable for families: "Yes, Puggles make GREAT family pets and are certainly suitable for families. They assimilate well into households with older children and existing pets. They love to be with their family during the day and snuggling in a lap at night.

I tend to encourage couples with small children to wait until their kids are 5+ years old before getting a puppy. Toddlers don't know their own strength and will often pick up and simply drop a pup if it nibbles or chews on them. The pup is not being mean or vicious but rather is feeling out his baby teeth on a new person. This can be hazardous for a very young pup as they can easily be hurt in the process of being dropped or squeezed.

So, yes, Puggles are a great addition to any family. Just make sure it is a wise time to introduce a four-legged family member to your home."

What Can I Do to Make My Puggle Love Me?

From the moment you bring your Puggle dog home, every minute you spend with him is an opportunity to bond. The earlier you start working with your dog, the more quickly that bond will grow and the closer you and your Puggle will become.

While simply spending time with your Puggle will encourage the growth of that bond, there are a few things you can do to purposefully build your bond with your dog. Some of these things include:

• Taking your Puggle for daily walks during which you frequently stop to pet and talk to your dog.

• Engaging your Puggle in games like fetch and hide-and-seek to encourage interaction.

• Interact with your dog through daily training sessions – teach your dog to pay attention when you say his name.

• Be calm and consistent when training your dog – always use positive reinforcement rather than punishment.

• Spend as much time with your Puggle as possible, even if

it means simply keeping the dog in the room with you while you cook dinner or pay bills.

Introductions With Other Pets

Introductions with other pets, especially with cats, often boil down to matters of territoriality. All dogs, by nature, defend their territory against intruders. From the Beagle side of the family, Puggles inherit a strongly protective territorial urge. Because they are part hound, Beagles are also prone to chase cats.

Neither of these behaviors does anything to facilitate a peace agreement with Fluffy. It's always best in a multi-pet household to let the animals work out the order of dominance in the family "pack" on their own if possible. To begin this process, create a neutral and controlled interaction under a closed bathroom door first.

Since cats are "weaponized" with an array of razor sharp claws, they can quickly put a puppy in his place. A swipe to the nose won't do a puppy any harm, but don't let things get out of hand. Oversee the first "in-person" meeting, but try not to overreact.

With other dogs in the house, you may want a more hands-on approach to the first "meet and greet." Always have two people present to control each dog. Make the introduction in a place that the older dog does not regard as "his." Even if the two dogs are going to be living in the same house, let them meet in neutral territory.

Keep your tone and demeanor calm, friendly, and happy. Let the dogs conduct the usual "sniff test," but don't let it go on for too long. Either dog may consider lengthy sniffing to be aggression.

Puppies may not yet understand the behavior of an adult dog and can be absolute little pests. If the puppy does get too "familiar," do not scold the older dog for issuing a warning snarl or growl.

A well-socialized older dog won't be displaying aggression with this reaction. He's just putting junior in his place and establishing the hierarchy of the pack

Be careful when you bring a new dog into the house not to neglect the older dog. Also be sure to spend time with him away from the puppy to assure your existing pet that your bond with him is strong and intact.

Exercise caution at meal times. Feed your pets in separate bowls so there is no perceived competition for food. (This is also a good policy to follow when introducing your puppy to the family cat.)

Habituation and Socialization

Habituation is when you continuously provide exposure to the same stimuli over a period of time. This will help your Puggle to relax in his environment and will teach him how to behave around unfamiliar people, noises, other pets, and different surroundings. Expose your Puggle puppy continuously to new sounds and new environments.

When you allow your Puggle to face life's positive experiences through socialization and habituation, you're helping your Puggle to build a library of valuable information that he can use when he's faced with a difficult situation. If he's had plenty of wonderful and positive early experiences, the more likely he'll be able to bounce back from any surprising or scary experiences.

When your Puggle puppy arrives at his new home for the first time, he'll start bonding with his human family immediately. This will be his primary bond. His secondary bond will be with everyone outside your home. A dog should never be secluded inside his home. Be sure to find the right balance where you're not exposing your Puggle puppy to too much external stimuli. If he starts becoming fearful, speak to your veterinarian.

The puppyhood journey can be tiresome yet very rewarding. Primary socialization starts between three and five weeks of age where a pup's experiences take place within his litter. This will have a huge impact on all his future emotional behavior.

Socialization from six to twelve weeks allows for puppies to bond with other species outside of their littermates and parents. It's at this particular stage that most pet parents will bring home a puppy and where he'll soon become comfortable with humans, other pets, and children.

By the time a puppy is around twelve to fourteen weeks, he becomes more difficult to introduce to new environments and new people and starts showing suspicion and distress. Nonetheless, if you've recently adopted a Puggle puppy or are bringing one home and he's beyond this ideal age, don't neglect to continue the socialization process. Puppies need to be exposed to as many new situations, environments, people, and other animals as possible, and it is never too late to start.

During puppyhood, you can easily teach your puppy to politely greet a new person, yet by the time a puppy has reached social maturity, the same puppy, if not properly socialized, may start lunging forward and acting aggressively, with the final outcome of lunging and nipping.

Never accidentally reward your Puggle puppy for displaying fear or growling at another dog or animal by picking them up. Picking up a Puggle puppy or dog at this time, when they are displaying unbalanced energy, actually turns out to be a reward for them, and you will be teaching them to continue with this type of behavior. As well, picking up a puppy literally places them in a "top dog" position where they are higher and more dominant than the dog or animal they just growled at.

The correct action to take in such a situation is to gently correct your puppy with a firm yet calm energy by distracting them with a "No," so that they learn to let you deal with the situation on their behalf.

If you allow a fearful or nervous puppy to deal with situations that unnerve them all by themselves, they may learn to react with fear or aggression, and you will have created a problem that could escalate into something quite serious as they grow older.

The same is true of situations where a young puppy may feel the need to protect themselves from a bigger or older dog that may come charging in for a sniff. It is the guardian's responsibility to protect the puppy so that they do not think they must react with fear or aggression in order to protect themselves.

Once your Puggle puppy has received all their vaccinations, you can take them out to public dog parks and various locations where many dogs are found.

Before allowing them to interact with other dogs or puppies, take them for a disciplined walk on leash so that they will be a little tired and less likely to immediately engage with all other dogs.

Keep your puppy on leash and close beside you, because most puppies are usually a bundle of out-of-control energy, and you need to protect them while teaching them how far they can go before getting themselves into trouble with adult dogs who may not appreciate excited puppy playfulness.

If your puppy shows any signs of aggression or domination toward another dog, you must immediately step in and calmly discipline them.

Take your puppy everywhere with you and introduce them to many different people of all ages, sizes, and ethnicities. Most people will come to you and want to interact with your puppy. If they ask if they can hold your puppy, let them, because so long as they are gentle and don't drop the puppy, this is a good way to socialize your Puggle and show them that humans are friendly.

As important as socialization is, it is also important that the dog be left alone for short periods when young so that they can cope with some periods of isolation. If an owner goes out and they have never experienced this, they can destroy things or make a mess because of panic. They are thinking they are vulnerable and can be attacked by something or someone coming in to the house.

Dogs that have been socialized are able to easily diffuse a potentially troublesome situation and hence they will rarely get into fights. Dogs that are poorly socialized often misinterpret or do not understand the subtle signals of other dogs, getting into trouble as a result.

Creating a Safe Environment

Never think for a minute that your Puggle would not bolt and run away. Even well-adjusted, happy puppies and adult dogs can run away, usually in extreme conditions such as with fireworks, thunder, or when scared.

Collar, tag, and microchip your new Puggle. Microchipping is not enough, since many pet parents tend to presume that dogs without collars are homeless or have been abandoned. Recent photos of your Puggle with the latest clip need to be placed in your wallet or purse.

Train your Puggle – foster and work with a professional, positive trainer to ensure that your Puggle does not run out the front door or out the backyard gate. Teach your Puggle basic, simple commands such as "come" and "stay."

Create a special, fun digging area just for him, hide his bones and toys and let your Puggle know that it's okay to dig in that area. After all, dogs need to play!

Introduce your new, furry companion to all your neighbors so everyone will know that he belongs to you.

Common Mistakes to Avoid

Never pick your Puggle puppy up if they are showing fear or aggression toward an object, another dog, or person, because this will be rewarding them for unbalanced behavior.

If they are doing something you do not want them to continue, your puppy needs to be gently corrected by you with firm and calm energy, so that they learn not to react with fear or aggression. When the mum of the litter tells her puppies off, she will use a deep noise with strong eye contact, until the puppy quickly realizes it's doing something naughty.

Don't play the "hand" game, where you slide the puppy across the floor with your hands because it's amusing for humans to see a little ball of fur scrambling to collect themselves and run back across the floor for another go.

This sort of "game" will teach your puppy to disrespect you as their leader in two different ways — first, because this "game" teaches them that humans are their play toys, and secondly, this type of "game" teaches them that humans are a source of excitement.

When your Puggle puppy is teething, they will naturally want to chew on everything within reach, and this will include you. As cute as you might think it is when they are young puppies, this is not an acceptable behavior, and you need to gently, but firmly, discourage the habit, just like a mother dog does to her puppies when they need to be weaned.

Always praise your puppy when they stop inappropriate behavior, as this is the beginning of teaching them to understand rules and boundaries. Often we humans are quick to discipline a puppy or dog for inappropriate behavior, but we forget to praise them for their good behavior.

Photo Credit: Mike & Tiffany Werner owners of Dexie & Morgan

Don't treat your Puggle like a small, furry human. When people try to turn dogs into people, this can cause them much stress and confusion that could lead to behavioral problems.

A well-behaved Puggle thrives on rules and boundaries, and when they understand that there is no question you are their leader and they are your follower, they will live a contented, happy, and stress-free life.

Dogs are a different species with different rules; for example, they do not naturally cuddle, and they need to learn to be stroked and cuddled by humans. Therefore, be careful when approaching a dog for the first time and being overly expressive with your hands. The safest areas to touch are the back and chest — avoid patting on the head and touching the ears.

Many people will assume that a dog that is yawning is tired — this is often a misinterpretation, and instead it is signaling your dog is uncomfortable and nervous about a situation.

Be careful when staring at dogs, because this is one of the ways in which they threaten each other. This body language can make them feel distinctly uneasy.

Puppy Nutrition

As dogs age, they thrive on a graduated program of nutrition. At age four months and less, puppies should get four small meals a day. From age 4-8 months, three meals per day are appropriate. From 8 months on, feed your pet twice a day.

Do not free feed (leave dry food out at all times) with a Puggle! They are as bad to beg and to overeat as their Pug parent. Do not allow a Puggle to become used to human food. The breed packs on the pounds quickly.

If you've ever had to try to slim down an obese pet, you know it is not an easy process! Thankfully, Puggles are playful and do like to run. Their exercise needs are minimal — about 30 minutes a day — but that activity and dietary control is crucial to forestall unhealthy weight gain.

Begin feeding your puppy by putting the food down for 10-20 minutes. If the dog doesn't eat, or only eats part of the serving, still take the bowl up. Don't give the dog more until the next scheduled feeding.

To give your puppy a good start in life, rely on high-quality, premium dry puppy food. If possible, replicate the puppy's existing diet. A sudden dietary switch can cause gastrointestinal upset. Maintain the dog's existing routine if practical. The vast majority of breeders recommend not feeding puppy food. It can be high in protein and actually can cause the puppy to grow too fast, thus possibly creating bone growth issues.

Before buying any dog food, read the label. The first listed ingredients should be meat, fishmeal, or whole grains. Foods with large amounts of fillers like cornmeal or meat by-products have a low nutritional value. They fill your dog up, but don't give him a range of vitamins and minerals, and they increase daily waste produced.

Wet foods are not appropriate for most growing dogs. They do not offer a good nutritional balance, and they are often upsetting to the stomach. Additionally, it's much harder to control portions with wet food, leading to young dogs being over or under fed. Controlling portions is important. Give your dog the amount stipulated on the food packaging for his weight and age, and nothing more.

Invest in weighted food and water bowls made out of stainless steel. The weights prevent the mess of "tip overs," and the material is much easier to clean than plastic. It does not hold odors or harbor bacteria.

Bowls in a stand that create an elevated feeding surface are also a good idea. Make sure your young dog can reach the food and water. Stainless steel bowl sets retail for less than $25 / £14.87.

Adult Nutrition

The same basic nutritional guidelines apply to adult Puggles. Always start with a high-quality, premium food. If possible, stay in the same product line the puppy received at the breeder. Graduated product lines help owners to create feeding programs that ensure nutritional consistency.

This approach allows you to transition your Puggle away from puppy food to an adult mixture, and in time to a senior formula. This removes the guesswork from nutritional management.

Say No to Table Scraps!

Dogs don't make it easy to say no when they beg at the table. If you let a puppy have so much as that first bite, you run the risk of creating a little tyrant – and one with an unhealthy habit.

(Even acceptable treats formulated for dogs should never comprise more than 5% of a dog's daily food intake.)

Table scraps contributes to weight problems, and many human foods are toxic to dogs. Dangerous items include, but are not limited to:

- Chocolate
- Raisins
- Alcohol
- Human vitamins (especially those with iron)
- Mushrooms
- Onions and garlic
- Walnuts
- Macadamia nuts
- Raw fish
- Raw pork

- Raw chicken

If you give your puppy a bone, watch him. Use only bones that are too large to choke on, and take the item away at the first sign of splintering. Commercial chew toys rated "puppy safe" are a much better option.

The Canine Teeth and Jaw

Even today, far too many dog food choices continue to have far more to do with being convenient for us humans to serve than they do with being a well-balanced, healthy food choice for a canine.

In order to choose the right food for your Puggle, first it's important to understand a little bit about canine physiology and what Mother Nature intended when she created our furry companions.

While humans are omnivores who can derive energy from eating plants, our canine companions are carnivores, which means they derive their energy and nutrient requirements from eating a diet consisting mainly or exclusively of the flesh of animals, birds, or fish.

Unlike humans, who are equipped with wide, flat molars for grinding grains, vegetables, and other plant-based materials, canine teeth are all pointed because they are designed to rip, shred, and tear into meat and bone.

Another obvious consideration when choosing an appropriate food source for our furry friends is the fact that every canine is born equipped with powerful jaws and neck muscles for the specific purpose of being able to pull down and tear apart their hunted prey.

The structure of the jaw of every canine is such that it opens widely to hold large pieces of meat and bone, while the mechanics of a dog's jaw permits only vertical (up and down) movement that is designed for crushing.

The Canine Digestive Tract

A dog's digestive tract is short and simple and designed to move their natural choice of food (hide, meat, and bone) quickly through their systems.

The canine digestive system is simply unable to properly break down vegetable matter, which is why whole vegetables look pretty much the same going into your dog as they do coming out the other end.

Given the choice, most dogs would never choose to eat plants and grains, or vegetables and fruits over meat, however, we humans continue to feed them a kibble-based diet that contains high amounts of vegetables, fruits, and grains with low amounts of meat.

Part of this is because we've been taught that it's a healthy, balanced diet for humans, and therefore, we believe that it must be the same for our dogs, and part of this is because all the fillers that make up our dog's food are less expensive and easier to process than meat.

How much healthier and long lived might our beloved Puggle be if, instead of largely ignoring nature's design for our canine companions, we chose to feed them whole, unprocessed, species-appropriate food with the main ingredient being meat?

Whatever you decide to feed your dog, keep in mind that just as too much wheat, other grains, and fillers in our human diet is having a detrimental effect on our health, the same can be very true for our best fur friends.

Our dogs are also suffering from many of the same life-threatening diseases that are rampant in our human society as a direct result of consuming a diet high in genetically altered, impure, processed, and packaged foods.

The BARF Diet

Raw feeding advocates believe that the ideal diet for their dog is one that would be very similar to what a dog living in the wild would have access to, and these canine guardians are often opposed to feeding their dog any sort of commercially manufactured pet foods.

On the other hand, those opposed to feeding their dogs a raw or Biologically Appropriate Raw Food (BARF) diet believe that the risks associated with food-borne illnesses during the handling and feeding of raw meats outweigh the purported benefits.

Raw meats purchased at your local grocery store contain a much higher level of acceptable bacteria than raw food produced for dogs, because the meat purchased for human consumption is meant to be cooked, which will kill any bacteria.

This means that canine guardians feeding their dogs a raw food diet can be quite certain that commercially prepared raw foods sold in pet stores will be safer than raw meats purchased in grocery stores.

Many guardians of high-energy, working breed dogs will agree that their dogs thrive on a raw or BARF diet and strongly believe that the potential benefits of feeding a dog a raw food diet are many, including:

- Healthy, shiny coats
- Decreased shedding
- Fewer allergy problems
- Healthier skin
- Cleaner teeth
- Fresher breath
- Higher energy levels
- Improved digestion
- Smaller stools
- Strengthened immune system
- Increased mobility in arthritic pets
- General increase or improvement in overall health

All dogs, whether working breed or lap dogs, are amazing athletes in their own right, therefore every dog deserves to be fed the best food available.

A raw diet is a direct evolution of what dogs ate before they became our domesticated pets and we turned toward commercially prepared, easy-to-serve dry dog food that required no special storage or preparation.

The Dehydrated Diet

Dehydrated dog food comes in both raw and cooked forms, and these foods are usually air-dried to reduce moisture to the level where bacterial growth is inhibited.

The appearance of dehydrated dog food is very similar to dry kibble, and the typical feeding methods include adding warm water before serving, which makes this type of diet both healthy for our dogs and convenient for us to serve.

Dehydrated recipes are made from minimally processed fresh whole foods to create a healthy and nutritionally balanced meal that will meet or exceed the dietary requirements for healthy canines.

Dehydrating removes only the moisture from the fresh ingredients, which usually means that because the food has not already been cooked at a high temperature, more of the overall nutrition is retained.

Photo Credit: Trevor Bowling owner of Samson

A dehydrated diet is a convenient way to feed your dog a nutritious diet, because all you have to do is add warm water and wait five minutes while the food re-hydrates so your Puggle can enjoy a warm meal.

The Kibble Diet

While many canine guardians are starting to take a closer look at the food choices they are making for their furry companions, there is no mistaking that the convenience and relative economy of dry dog food kibble, which had its beginnings in the 1940s, continues to be the most popular pet food choice for most humans.

While feeding a high-quality, bagged kibble diet that has been flavored to appeal to dogs and supplemented with vegetables and fruits to appeal to humans may keep most every Puggle companion happy and healthy, you will need to decide whether this is the best diet for them.

Your Puppy's First Lessons

Don't give a young dog full run of the house before the puppy is house trained. Keep your new pet confined to a designated area behind a baby gate. This protects your home and possessions and keeps the dog safe from hazards like staircases. Depending on the size and configuration, baby gates retail from $25-$100 / £14.87-£59.46. During those times when you are not home to supervise the puppy, crate your pet.

Housebreaking

Crate training and housebreaking go hand in hand. Puggles, like all dogs, come to see their crate as their den. They will hold their need to urinate or defecate while they are inside. Any time you leave the house, you should crate your pet, immediately taking the dog out upon your return.

Establishing and maintaining a daily routine also helps your dog in this respect. Feed your pet at the same time each day, taking him out afterwards. The feeding schedule dictates the frequency of "relief" breaks. Trips "out" will also decrease as the dog ages.

Don't be rigid in holding your puppy to this standard. Puppies have less control over their bladder and bowel movements than adult dogs. They need to go out more often, especially after they've been active or gotten excited.

On average, adult dogs go out 3-4 times a day: when they wake up, within an hour of eating, and right before bedtime. With puppies, don't wait more than 15 minutes after a meal.
Praise your pet with the same phrases to encourage and reinforces good elimination habits.

Use positive reinforcement and encouraging phrases to support correct elimination habits. Do not punish a dog for an accident. Your pet does not have the ability to associate the punishment with the incident. Your anger will leave him uncomfortable and anxious. He'll know he did something wrong, but he won't understand what.

If you catch your dog in the act of eliminating in the house, say "bad dog" in a stern, firm voice, but do not belabor the point. Clean up the accident using an enzymatic cleaner to eradicate the odor and return to the dog's normal routine. Nature's Miracle Stain and Odor Removal is an excellent product and affordable at $5 / £2.97 per 32 ounce / 0.9 liter bottle.

The following are methods that you may or may not have considered, all of which have their own merits, including:

• Bell training
• Exercise pen training
• Free training
• Kennel training

All of these are effective methods, so long as you add in the one critical and often missing "wild card" ingredient, which is "human training."

When you bring home your new Puggle puppy, they will be relying upon your guidance to teach them what they need to learn, and when it comes to housetraining, the first thing the human guardian needs to learn is that the puppy is not being bad when they pee or poop inside.

They are just responding to the call of Mother Nature, and you need to pay close attention right from the very beginning, because it's entirely possible to teach a puppy to go to the bathroom outside in less than a week. Therefore, if your puppy is making bathroom "mistakes," blame yourself, not your puppy.

Check in with yourself and make sure your energy remains consistently calm and patient and that you exercise plenty of compassion and understanding while you help your new puppy learn the bathroom rules. Don't clean up after your puppy with them watching, as this makes the puppy believe you are there to clean up after them, making you lower in the dog pack order.

While your puppy is still growing, on average, they can hold it approximately one hour for every month of their age. This means that if your 3-month-old puppy has been happily snoozing for two to three hours, as soon as they wake up, they will need to go outside.

Some of the first indications or signs that your puppy needs to be taken outside to relieve themselves will be when you see them:

• Sniffing around
• Circling
• Looking for the door
• Whining, crying or barking
• Acting agitated

During the early stages of potty training, adding treats as an extra incentive can be a good way to reinforce how happy you are that your puppy is learning to relieve themselves in the right place. Slowly, treats can be removed and replaced with your happy praise, or you can give your puppy a treat after they are back inside.

Next, now that you have a new puppy in your life, you will want to be flexible with respect to adapting your schedule to meet their internal clocks to quickly teach your Puggle puppy their new bathroom routine.

This means not leaving your puppy alone for endless hours at a time, because firstly, they are pack animals that need companionship and your direction at all times, and secondly, long periods alone will result in the disruption of the potty training schedule you have worked hard to establish.

If you have no choice but to leave your puppy alone for many hours, make sure that you place them in a paper-lined room or pen where they can relieve themselves without destroying your newly installed hardwood or favorite carpet.

Remember, your Puggle is a growing puppy with a bladder and bowels that they do not yet have complete control over.

Breeder Mo DeVille of PuggleUK has these tips: "Our Puggles are quite sensitive in nature and hate getting things wrong. Their objective in life is to please. The best of our pups get the house breaking in ONE day - most within two weeks. Understand that you have a BABY animal. Take it outside when it wakes up (at any time of the day), after feeding, after playing, after ANY stimulation, on the hour, every hour. As the puppy has a wee or does its business, say a specific word or, if you are clicker training, click then reward the puppy with praise. Sooner than you think, your puppy will start to react to you using the word and do whatever action you want it to do. (To encourage our dogs to wee we say 'Be quick.') The puppy will be so pleased with itself for getting it right! Remember to choose a word you are happy saying in public places though!"

Photo Credit: Puggle is Lexie by Ashley Edward Steinbach

Bell Training

A very easy way to introduce your new Puggle puppy to house training is to begin by teaching them how to ring a doorbell whenever they need to go outside. A further benefit of training your puppy to ring a bell is that you will not have to listen to your puppy or dog whining, barking, or howling to be let out, and your door will not become scratched up from their nails.

Attach the bell to a piece of ribbon or string and hang it from a door handle or tape it to a doorsill near the door where you will be taking your puppy out when they need to relieve themselves. The string will need to be long enough so that your puppy can easily reach the bell with their nose or a paw.

Next, each time you take your puppy out to relieve themselves, say the word "out," and use their paw or their nose to ring the bell. Praise them for this "trick" and immediately take them outside. This type of an alert system is an easy way to eliminate accidents in the home.

Kennel Training

When you train your Puggle puppy to accept sleeping in their own kennel at nighttime, this will also help to accelerate their potty training. Because no puppy or dog wants to relieve themselves where they sleep, they will hold their bladder and bowels as long as they possibly can.

Presenting them with familiar scents by taking them to the same spot in the yard or the same street corner will help to remind and encourage them that they are outside to relieve themselves. Use a voice cue to remind your puppy why they are outside, such as "go pee," and always remember to praise them every time they relieve themselves in the right place, so that they quickly understand what you expect of them.

Exercise Pen Training

The exercise pen is a transition from kennel-only training and will be helpful for those times when you may have to leave your Puggle puppy for more hours than they can reasonably be expected to hold it.

Exercise pens are usually constructed of wire sections that you can put together in whatever shape you desire, and the pen needs to be large enough to hold your puppy's kennel in one half of the pen, while the other half will be lined with newspapers or pee pads.

Place your Puggle puppy's food and water dishes next to the kennel and leave the kennel door open (or take it off), so they can wander in and out whenever they wish to eat or drink or go to the papers or pee pads if they need to relieve themselves.

Because they are already used to sleeping inside their kennel, they will not want to relieve themselves inside the area where they sleep. Therefore, your puppy will naturally go to the other half of the pen to relieve themselves on the newspapers or pee pads.

Free Training

If you would rather not confine your young Puggle puppy to one or two rooms in your home and will be allowing them to freely range about your home anywhere they wish during the day, this is considered free training.

Never get upset or scold a puppy for having an accident inside the home, because this will result in teaching your puppy to be afraid of you and to only relieve themselves in secret places or when you're not watching.

If you catch your Puggle puppy making a mistake, all that is necessary is for you to calmly say "no," quickly scoop them up, and take them outside or to their indoor bathroom area.

The Puggle will generally do very well when you start them off with "puppy pee pads" that you will move closer and closer to the same door that you always use when taking them outside.

This way, they will quickly learn to associate going to this door with when they need to relieve themselves.

Marking Territory

Both male and female dogs with intact reproductive systems mark territory by urinating. This is most often an outdoor behavior, but can happen inside if the dog is upset. Again, use an enzymatic cleaner to remove the odor and minimize the attractiveness of the location to the dog. Territory marking is especially prevalent in intact males. The obvious long-term solution is to have the dog neutered.

Marking territory is not a consequence of poor house training. The behavior can be seen in dogs that would otherwise never "go" in the house. It stems from completely different urges and reactions.

Dealing With Separation Anxiety

Separation anxiety manifests in a variety of ways, ranging from vocalizations to nervous chewing. Dogs that are otherwise well trained may urinate or defecate in the house.

These behaviors begin when your Puggle recognizes signs that you are leaving. Triggers include picking up a set of car keys or putting on a coat. The dog may start to follow you around the house trying to get your attention, jumping up on you or otherwise trying to touch you.

It is imperative that you understand when you adopt a Puggle that they are companion dogs. They must have time to connect and be with their humans. You are the center of your dog's world. The behavior that a dog exhibits when it has separation anxiety is not a case of the animal being "bad." The poor thing experiences real distress and loneliness.

The purpose of crate training is not to punish or imprison a dog. It is not a cruel or repressive measure. The crate is the dog's "safe place" and is a great coping mechanism for breeds with separation anxiety issues. You are not being mean or cruel teaching your dog to stay in a crate when you are away – you are *helping* your Puggle to cope.

Breeder Mo DeVille of PuggleUK advises: "Separation anxiety can start right at the beginning of the puppy's life with you if you don't get the initial introduction to crate training right. I recommend that once the family has arrived home with their new puppy, they take it straight outside to relieve itself – that is so that its first introduction to the home isn't as a bathroom! Play with it, feed it, take it outside again and then, put it in its crate. No doubt the pup will make a fuss about being put in there but, for as long as it takes for the pup to calm down and go off to sleep (as it will surely do) nobody is to look at it, talk to it, or fuss it. The puppy doesn't understand your words, just that it has elicited a reaction from you. Carry on with your normal chores, walk past the crate, keep on with your life but IGNORE the pup. It isn't alone as it has the comfort of you being around (other pets should be kept away for this first introduction) but, as it doesn't get a reaction from you, it will soon get bored and go to sleep. An absolute NO is to get the puppy home and only put it in its crate when you are about to abandon it and go to bed. It will feel abandoned, frightened, and will, undoubtedly, shout the house down in its anguish!"

Grooming

Do not allow yourself to get caught in the "my Puggle doesn't like it" trap, which is an excuse many owners will use to avoid regular grooming sessions. When you allow your dog to dictate whether they will permit a grooming session, you are setting a dangerous precedent.

Once you have bonded with your dog, they love to be tickled, rubbed, and scratched in certain favorite places. This is why grooming is a great source of pleasure and a way to bond with your pet.

Puggles shed moderately for most of the year, but heavily when the weather begins to turn warm. Brush once a week until shedding season, then daily to get all the loose hair out of the coat.

The best option is a bristle brush, which works well with all coats from long to short. These brushes remove dirt and debris and distribute natural oils throughout the coat. A good quality bristle brush costs less than $15 / £9 and often less than $10 / £6.

Photo Credit: John & Margie Couch of Hugapuggle

Grooming/brushing sessions are an excellent opportunity to examine your dog's skin. Look for any growths, lumps, bumps, or wounds. Also have a good look at his ears, eyes, and mouth. Vigilant prevention is the hallmark of good healthcare for all companion animals. Watch for any discharge from the eyes or ears, as well accumulated debris in the ear canal and a foul or yeasty odor. (This is a sign of parasitical mite activity.)

Nail Trimming

Coat maintenance is not the only grooming chore necessary to keep your Puggle in good shape. Even dogs that walk on asphalt or other rough surfaces often will need to have their nails trimmed from time to time.

If your pet is agreeable, this is a job you can perform at home with a trimmer especially designed for use with dogs. I prefer those with plier grips. They're easier to handle and quite cost effective, selling for under $20 / £11.88

Even better than a nail clipper is the electric Dremel™ tool since there is a lesser chance of cutting into the quick. In addition, your dog's nails will be smooth, without the sharp edges clipping alone can create.

NOTE: never use a regular Dremel™ tool, as it will be too high speed and will burn your dog's toenails. Only use a slow speed Dremel™, such as Model 7300-PT Pet Nail Grooming Tool (approx. $40/£20). You can also purchase the flexible hose attachment for the Dremel, which is much easier to handle and can be held like a pencil.

Snip off the nail tips at a 45-degree angle, being careful not to cut too far down. If you do, you'll catch the vascular quick, which will hurt the dog and cause heavy bleeding. If you are apprehensive about performing this chore, ask your vet tech or groomer to walk you through it the first time.

Bathing

One bath per month should suffice for a Puggle, unless the dog has gotten into something. More frequent bathing may dry out or irritate the skin, especially in the winter months. Avoid getting water on the dog's head, which can cause ear infections and allow moisture to accumulate in the facial wrinkles, which are a prime location for fungal growth.

For "do it yourself" bathing, clean the head and face with a warm, wet washcloth only. Rinse your dog's coat with clean, fresh water to remove all residues. Dry your pet thoroughly with a towel to remove as much loose hair as possible. Be sure to use a thin washcloth or folded gauze to dry the skin folds and creases on the face.

If you opt to work with a professional groomer, the services are typically quite reasonable for a breed with this coat type, falling in a range of $25-$50 / £15-£30 per session.

One tip is to use Chamois cloths to dry the Puggle. It works great and they don't have to be laundered as much. They just air dry, and can be washed in the washing machine. However, DO NOT put in the dryer. I have found that they work much better than towels.

Anal Glands

All dogs can suffer from blocked anal glands. The dog may scoot or rub its bottom on the ground or carpet. (You may also notice a foul odor.)

If this occurs, the glands will need expressing to prevent an abscess from forming. This is a sensitive task and one that a veterinarian or an experienced groomer should perform.

Fleas And Ticks

I'm including fleas and ticks under grooming because that's when they're usually found. Don't think that if your Puggle has "passengers" you're doing something wrong, or that the dog is at fault. This is a part of dog ownership. Sooner or later, it will happen. Address the problem, but don't "freak out."

Do NOT use a commercial flea product on a puppy of less than 12 weeks of age, and be extremely careful with adult dogs. Most of the major products contain pyrethrum. The chemical causes long-term neurological damage and even fatalities in small dogs.

To get rid of fleas, bathe your dog in warm water with a standard canine shampoo. Comb the animal's fur with a fine-toothed flea comb, which will trap the live parasites. Submerge the comb in hot soapy water to kill the fleas.

Wash the dog's bedding and any soft materials with which he has come in contact. Look for any accumulations of "flea dirt," which is blood excreted by adult fleas. Wash the bedding and other surfaces daily for at least a week to kill any remaining eggs before they hatch.

If you find a tick, coat it with a thick layer of petroleum jelly for 5 minutes to suffocate the parasite and cause its jaws to release. Pluck the tick off with a pair of tweezers using a straight motion.

Never simply jerk a tick off a dog. The parasite's head stays behind and continues to burrow into the skin, making a painful sore.

Managing Your Pug's Activity

Puggles are incredibly energetic, playing hard and crashing equally hard. Channel that energy into appropriate chew toys, training classes, and walks. The dogs settle down as they age, but you don't want any leftover bad habits from puppyhood.

Puggles are very cute when they howl, but don't let that behavior get started, especially by joining in yourself. Your dog already sees you as part of his pack (hopefully as the leader of the group) and will think howling at the moon is a shared behavior. You may think it's adorable, but the neighbors won't!

As adults, Puggles do fine with two 15-minute walks per day. They are alert, interested dogs that will take note of everything going on around them. Be sure to crate train your Puggle because the breed is known to suffer from separation anxiety.

Photo Credit: PuggleBaby.com and owner Rachael Remijn

Collar or Harness?

Regardless of breed, I'm not a big fan of using a traditional collar. I wouldn't enjoy a choking sensation and assume my dog wouldn't either. My current favorite on-body restraints are the harnesses that look like vests. They offer a point of attachment for the lead on the back between the shoulders.

This arrangement directs pressure away from the neck and allows for easy, free movement. Young dogs are less resistant to this system and don't strain against a harness the way they will with a collar.

It's best to take your dog with you to the pet store to get a proper fit. Sizing for a dog is much more unpredictable than you might think. I have seen dogs as large as 14 lbs. / 6.35 kg take an "Extra Small" depending on their build. Regardless of size, harnesses retail in a range of $20 - $25 / £11.88 - £14.85

Standard Leash or Retractable?

The decision to buy a standard, fixed-length leash or a retractable lead is, for the most part, a matter of personal preference. Some facilities like groomers, vet clinics, and dog daycares ask that you not use a retractable lead on their premises. The long line represents a trip and fall hazard for other human clients.

Fixed-length leashes often sell for as little as $5 / £2.97, while retractable leads are less than $15 / £8.91.

Learning to respond to your control of the leash is an important behavioral lesson for your Puggles. Do not drag a dog on a lead or jerk him. If your pet sits down and refuses to budge, pick him up. Don't let the dog be in charge of the walk or you'll have the devil's own time regaining the upper hand.

Puggles are scent dogs thanks to their Beagle parent. They love to get out in the world and "sniff the trail." They will associate the lead with adventures and time with you. Don't be at all surprised if your dog picks up words associated with excursions like go, out, car, drive, or walk and responds accordingly.

Never let a Puggle off the leash in an open, unfenced area! They run like the wind and don't come when they are called, especially when they are chasing down an interesting scent.

Dog Walking Tips

Teach your dog to "sit" by using the word and making a downward pointing motion with your finger or indicating the desired direction with the palm of your hand. Do not attach the lead until your dog complies.

If your puppy jerks or pulls on the leash, stop, pick up the dog, and start the walk over with the "sit" command. Make it clear that the walk ceases when the dog misbehaves.

Praise your dog for walking well on the end of the lead and for stopping when you stop. Reinforce positive behaviors during walks. Your dog will get the message and show the same traits during other activities.

The Importance of Basic Commands

It is to your advantage to go through a basic obedience class with your dog. Puggles are intelligent, but stubborn dogs. All dogs respond well to a consistent routine and to a command "language." Provide both of these vital foundations to have a well-behaved pet.

Experts agree that most dogs can pick up between 165 and 200 words, but they can't extrapolate more than one meaning. If, for instance, your dog barks, you need to use the same "command" in response, like "quiet." If he picks something up, you might say "drop it."

For problem jumping, most owners go with "down." The point is to pick a set of words and use them over and over again to create a basic vocabulary for your dog. Both the word and your tone of voice should convey your authority and elicit the desired response.

Investigate enrollment in an obedience class through your local big box pet store, or ask your vet about trainers in your area. It is to your advantage if you can locate a trainer who has experience with the breed. Start the lessons early in your dog's life by offering him the stability of consistent reactions.

Play Time and Tricks

Puggles are not known to be easy to train, but they are companionable dogs and considered to be quite smart. Give your pet plenty of toys, and observe what he does and doesn't like to do before you start thinking about teaching him tricks.

Don't select toys that are soft and "shred-able." I recommend chew toys like Nylabones that can withstand the abuse. You can buy items made out of this tough material in the $1-$5 / £0.59-£2.97 range.

Never give your dog rawhide or pig's ears, which soften and present a choking hazard. Also avoid cow hooves, which can splinter and puncture the cheek or palate.

Avoid soft rubber toys. They shred into small pieces, which the dog will swallow. Opt for rope toys instead. Don't buy anything with a squeaker or any other part that presents a choking hazard.

Your dog will learn a basic set of commands like sit, stay, heel, and so forth in his obedience training. These commands can be used as the basis to get your dog to respond to cues to perform tricks. Some Puggles are agreeable to the process, and others just walk away. It certainly doesn't hurt to try, but never try to force your pet to do something he really doesn't want to do.

Playtime is important, especially for a dog's natural desire to chase. Try channeling this instinct with toys and games. If a dog has no stimulation and has nothing to chase, they can start to chase their own tail, which can lead to problems.

Toys can be used to simulate the dog's natural desire to hunt. For example, when they catch a toy, they will often shake it and bury their teeth into it, simulating the killing of their prey.

Allow your dog to fulfill a natural desire to chew. This comes from historically catching their prey and then chewing the carcass. Providing chews or bones can prevent your dog from destroying your home.

Playing with your dog is not only a great way of getting them to use up their energy, but it is also a great way of bonding with them as they have fun. Dogs love to chase and catch balls, just make sure that the ball is too large to be swallowed.

Deer antlers are wonderful toys for Puggles. Most love them. They do not smell, are all-natural, and do not stain or splinter. I recommend the antlers that are not split as they last longer.

Dogs that don't get enough exercise are also more likely to develop problem behaviors like chewing, digging, and barking.

Chapter 6 - Training and Correcting Problem Behaviors

Puggles love to play. They're intelligent and fun, but like any breed can also become spoiled little tyrants. Separation anxiety is an issue with this breed, so crate training from an early age is essential. This will also facilitate the housebreaking process, which can be protracted (as long as six months.)

Photo Credit: Trevor Bowling owner of Samson

Negative behavior may not target humans. Puggles can be aggressive, especially when they are acting on their territorial urge to protect items they see as their possessions, including their crate, and their home ground — your house.

Typically, they warm up fine to strangers after a little initial barking, but like many smaller breeds, it may be your Puggle that starts a confrontation with another dog by snapping, lunging, pushing, barking, or baring its teeth. Thankfully, Puggles have a good reputation for positive interaction with other dogs, but they do often like to chase cats.

Take your puppy to a training class. Introduce him to new sights, sounds, people, and places. Let him interact with other dogs in a controlled environment. There, the dog is safe to deal with fear and timidity without blustering self-defense postures. You'll get a better-mannered dog and a greater understanding of how to guide your pet's future interactions.

Responsible dog owners are attentive to the behavior of their own dog and to what's going on around them. They praise good behavior, but accept responsibility for anticipating potential clashes. Often in a public setting, the wisest course of action is to avoid a meeting with another dog altogether.

In the last chapter, I discussed leash training, which is crucial for successful public outings. Rather than avoiding areas with other people and dogs, your goal is to be able to take your dog to such places without incident. Contrary to what some people think, well-managed outings in varied environments help to create confidence in your dog.

Breeder Mo DeVille of PuggleUK says: "When training your puppy, use its name as a 'tap on the shoulder' to attract its attention. Repeatedly calling its name will get you nowhere. Teach it to come to you with a command – 'Rufus, come!' 'Rufus, sit!' – and always reward and accentuate the positive. We have been breeding this enchanting little dog since 2006 and have absolutely no regrets about welcoming them into our lives. Enjoy your Puggle and remember: it is intelligent, trainable, funny, loving, and has a wicked sense of humor that, sometimes, will outwit you!"

Dog Whisperer or Trainer?

Many people can be confused when they need professional help with their dog, because for many years, if you needed help with your dog, you contacted a "dog trainer" or took your dog to "puppy classes" where your dog would learn how to sit or stay.

The difference between a dog trainer and a dog whisperer would be that a "dog trainer" teaches a dog how to perform certain tasks, and a "dog whisperer" alleviates behavior problems by teaching humans what they need to do to keep their particular dog happy.

Often, depending on how soon the guardian has sought help, this can mean that the dog in question has developed some pretty serious issues, such as aggressive barking, lunging, biting, or attacking other dogs, pets, or people.

Dog whispering is often an emotional roller coaster ride for the humans involved that unveils many truths when they finally realize that it has been their actions (or inactions) that have likely caused the unbalanced behavior that their dog is now displaying.

Once solutions are provided, the relief for both dog and human can be quite cathartic when they realize that with the correct direction, they can indeed live a happy life with their dog.

All specific methods of training, such as "clicker training," fall outside of what every dog needs to be happy, because training your dog to respond to a clicker, which you can easily do on your own, and then letting them sleep in your bed, eat from your plate, and any other multitude of things humans allow, are what makes the dog unbalanced and causes behavior problems.

I always say to people, don't wait until you have a severe problem before getting some dog whispering or professional help of some sort, because "With the proper training, Man can learn to be dog's best friend."

Don't Reward Unwanted Behavior

It is very important to recognize that any attention paid to an out-of-control, adolescent puppy, even negative attention, is likely to be exciting and rewarding for your Puggle puppy.

Chasing after a puppy when they have taken something they shouldn't have, picking them up when barking or showing aggression, pushing them off when they jump on other people, or yelling when they refuse to come when called are all forms of attention that can actually be rewarding for most puppies. It will be your responsibility to provide structure for your puppy, which will include finding acceptable and safe ways to allow your puppy to vent their energy without being destructive or harmful to others.

The worst thing you can do when training your Puggle is to yell at him or use punishment. Positive reinforcement training methods – that is, rewarding your dog for good behavior – are infinitely more effective than negative reinforcement – training by punishment. It is important when training your Puggle that you do not allow yourself to get frustrated. If you feel yourself starting to get angry, take a break and come back to the training session later.

Why is punishment-based training so bad? Think about it this way – your dog should listen to you because he wants to please you, right? If you train your dog using punishment, he could become fearful of you, and that could put a damper on your relationship with him. Do your dog and yourself a favor by using positive reinforcement.

Teaching Basic Commands

When it comes to training your Puggle, you have to start off slowly with the basic commands. The most popular basic commands for dogs include sit, down, stay, and come.

Sit

This is the most basic and one of the most important commands you can teach your Puggle.

1.)   Stand in front of your Puggle with a few small treats in your pocket.

2.)   Hold one treat in your dominant hand and wave it in front of your Puggle's nose so he gets the scent.

3.)   Give the "Sit" command.

4.)   Move the treat upward and backward over your Puggle's head so he is forced to raise his head to follow it.

5.)   In the process, his bottom will lower to the ground.

6.)   As soon as your Puggle's bottom hits the ground, praise him and give him the treat.

7.)   Repeat this process several times until your dog gets the hang of it and responds consistently.

Down

After the "Sit" command, "Down" is the next logical command to teach because it is a progression from "Sit."

1.)   Kneel in front of your Puggle with a few small treats in your pocket.

2.)   Hold one treat in your dominant hand and give your Puggle the "Sit" command.

3.)   Reward your Puggle for sitting, then give him the "Down" command.

4.)   Quickly move the treat down to the floor between your Puggle's paws.

5.)   Your dog will follow the treat and should lie down to retrieve it.

6.)   Praise and reward your Puggle when he lies down.

7.)   Repeat this process several times until your dog gets the hang of it and responds consistently.

Come

It is very important that your Puggle responds to a "Come" command, because there may come a time when you need to get his attention and call him to your side during a dangerous situation (such as him running around too close to traffic).

1.)   Put your Puggle on a short leash and stand in front of him.

2.)   Give your Puggle the "Come" command, then quickly take a few steps backward away from him.

3.)   Clap your hands and act excited, but do not repeat the "Come" command.

4.)   Keep moving backwards in small steps until your Puggle follows and comes to you.

5.)   Praise and reward your Puggle and repeat the process.

6.)   Over time, you can use a longer leash or take your Puggle off the leash entirely.

7.)   You can also start by standing farther from your Puggle when you give the "Come" command.

8.)   If your Puggle doesn't come to you immediately, you can use the leash to pull him toward you.

Stay

This command is very important because it teaches your Puggle discipline – not only does it teach your Puggle to stay, but it also forces him to listen and pay attention to you.

1.)   Find a friend to help you with this training session.

2.)   Have your friend hold your Puggle on the leash while you stand in front of the dog.

3.)   Give your Puggle the "Sit" command and reward him for responding correctly.

4.)   Give your dog the "Stay" command while holding your hand out like a stop sign.

5.)   Take a few steps backward away from your dog and pause for 1 to 2 seconds.

6.)   Step back toward your Puggle, then praise and reward your dog.

7.)   Repeat the process several times, then start moving back a little farther before you return to your dog.

Beyond Basic Training

Once your Puggle has a firm grasp on the basics, you can move on to teaching him additional commands. You can also add distractions to the equation to reinforce your dog's mastery of the commands. The goal is to ensure that your Puggle responds to your command each and every time – regardless of distractions and anything else he might rather be doing. This is incredibly important, because there may come a time when your dog is in a dangerous situation and if he doesn't respond to your command, he could get hurt.

If you previously conducted your training sessions indoors, you might consider moving them outside where your dog could be distracted by various sights, smells, and sounds.

One thing you might try is to give your dog the Stay command and then toss a toy nearby that will tempt him to break his Stay. Start by tossing the toy at a good distance from him and wait a few seconds before you release him to play.

Eventually you will be able to toss a toy right next to your dog without him breaking his Stay until you give him permission to do so.

Incorporating Hand Signals

Teaching your Puggle to respond to hand signals in addition to verbal commands is very useful – you never know when you will be in a situation where your dog might not be able to hear you.

To start out, choose your dominant hand to give the hand signals, and hold a small treat in that hand while you are training your dog – this will encourage your dog to focus on your hand during training, and it will help to cement the connection between the command and the hand signal.

To begin, give your dog the Sit or Down command while holding the treat in your dominant hand and give the appropriate hand signal – for Sit you might try a closed fist, and for Down, you might place your hand flat, parallel to the ground.

When your dog responds correctly, give him the treat. You will need to repeat this process many times in order for your dog to form a connection between both the verbal command and the hand signal with the desired behavior.

Eventually, you can start to remove the verbal command from the equation – use the hand gesture every time, but start to use the verbal command only half the time.

Once your dog gets the hang of this, you should start to remove the food reward from the equation. Continue to give your dog the hand signal for each command, and occasionally use the verbal command just to remind him.

You should start to phase out the food rewards, however, by offering them only half the time. Progressively lessen the use of the food reward, but continue to praise your dog for performing the behavior correctly so he learns to repeat it.

Teaching Distance Commands

In addition to getting your dog to respond to hand signals, it is also useful to teach him to respond to your commands even when you are not directly next to him.

This may come in handy if your dog is running around outside and gets too close to the street – you should be able to give him a Sit or Down command so he stops before he gets into a dangerous situation.

Teaching your dog distance commands is not difficult, but it does require some time and patience.

To start, give your Puggle a brief refresher course of the basic commands while you are standing or kneeling right next to him.

Next, give your dog the Sit and Stay commands, then move a few feet away before you give the Come command.

Repeat this process, increasing the distance between you and your dog before giving him the Come command. Be sure to praise and reward your dog for responding appropriately when he does so.

Once your dog gets the hang of coming on command from a distance, you can start to incorporate other commands.

One method is to teach your dog to sit when you grab his collar. To do so, let your dog wander freely and every once in a while walk up and grab his collar while giving the Sit command.

After a few repetitions, your dog should begin to respond with a Sit when you grab his collar, even if you do not give the command.

Gradually, you can increase the distance from which you come to grab his collar and give him the command.

Photo Credit: Murlin from Rebecca Youngbar

After your dog starts to respond consistently when you come from a distance to grab his collar, you can start giving the Sit command without moving toward him.

It may take your dog a few times to get the hang of it, so be patient. If your dog doesn't sit right away, calmly walk up to him and repeat the Sit command, but do not grab his collar this time. Eventually, your dog will get the hang of it, and you can start to practice using other commands like Down and Stay from a distance.

Clicker Training

When it comes to training your Puggle, you are going to be most successful if you maintain consistency. Puggles have a tendency to be a little stubborn, so unless you are very clear with your dog about what your expectations are, he may simply decide not to follow your commands.

A simple way to achieve consistency in training your Puggle is to use the principles of clicker training. Clicker training involves using a small handheld device that makes a clicking noise when you press it between your fingers.

Clicker training is based on the theory of operant conditioning, which helps your dog to make the connection between the desired behavior and the offering of a reward.

Puggles have a natural desire to please, so if they learn that a certain behavior earns your approval, they will be eager to repeat it – clicker training is a great way to help your dog quickly identify the particular behavior you want him to repeat.

All you have to do is give your Puggle a command, and as soon as he performs the behavior, you use the clicker. After you use the clicker, give your dog the reward as you would with any form of positive reinforcement training. Benefits include:

•   Very easy to implement – all you need is the clicker.

- Helps your dog form a connection between the command and the desired behavior more quickly.
- You only need to use the clicker until your dog makes the connection, then you can stop.
- May help to keep your dog's attention more effectively if he hears the noise.

Clicker training is just one method of positive reinforcement training that you can consider for training your Puggle. No matter what method you choose, it is important that you maintain consistency and always praise and reward him for responding to your commands correctly, so he learns to repeat the behavior.

First Tricks

When teaching your Puggle their first tricks, in order to give them extra incentive, find a small treat that they would do anything to get, and give the treat as a reward to help solidify a good performance.

Most dogs will be extra attentive during training sessions when they know that they will be rewarded with their favorite treats.

If your Puggle is less than six months old when you begin teaching them tricks, keep your training sessions short (no more than 5 or 10 minutes) and make the sessions lots of fun. As your Puggle becomes an adult, you can extend your sessions, because they will be able to maintain their focus for longer periods of time.

Shake a Paw

Who doesn't love a dog who knows how to shake a paw? This is one of the easiest tricks to teach your Puggle. Practice every day until they are 100% reliable with this trick, and then it will be time to add another trick to their repertoire.

Most dogs are naturally either right or left pawed. If you know which paw your dog favors, ask them to shake this paw.

Find a quiet place to practice, without noisy distractions or other pets, and stand or sit in front of your dog. Place them in the sitting position and hold a treat in your left hand.

Say the command "Shake" while putting your right hand behind their left or right paw and pulling the paw gently toward yourself until you are holding their paw in your hand. Immediately praise them and give them the treat.

Most dogs will learn the "Shake" trick very quickly, and in no time at all, once you put out your hand, your Puggle will immediately lift their paw and put it into your hand, without your assistance or any verbal cue.

Give Me Five

The next trick after "Shake" should be "High Five." Teach this sequence the same way, but when you hold out your hand to shake, move your hand up and touch your dog's paw saying, "High Five!" It may take a few tries, but by this time your Puggle will be getting the idea that if he learns his lessons, he gets his treat.

This pair of tricks is a good example of using one behavior to build to another. Almost any dog can be taught to perform basic tricks, but don't lose sight of the fact that you are dealing with an individual personality. You may have a Puggle that would rather chase his chew toys than learn "routines."

Get to know what your dog enjoys doing and follow his lead to build his unique set of tricks.

Roll Over

You will find that just like your Puggle is naturally either right or left pawed, that they will also naturally want to roll either to the right or to the left side.

Take advantage of this by asking your dog to roll to the side they naturally prefer. Sit with your dog on the floor and put them in a lying down position.

Hold a treat in your hand and place it close to their nose without allowing them to grab it, and while they are in the lying position, move the treat to the right or left side of their head so that they have to roll over to get to it.

You will quickly see to which side they want to roll naturally; once you see this, move the treat to that side. Once they roll over to that side, immediately give them the treat and praise them.

You can say the verbal cue "Over" while you demonstrate the hand signal motion (moving your right hand in a half circular motion) from one side of their head to the other.

Sit Pretty

While this trick is a little more complicated, and most dogs pick up on it very quickly, remember that this trick requires balance, and every dog is different, so always exercise patience.

Find a quiet space with few distractions and sit or stand in front of your dog and ask them to "Sit."

Have a treat nearby (on a countertop or table) and when they sit, use both of your hands to lift up their front paws into the sitting pretty position, while saying the command "Sit Pretty." Help them balance in this position while you praise them and give them the treat.

Once your Puggle can do the balancing part of the trick quite easily without your help, sit or stand in front of your dog while asking them to "Sit Pretty" and hold the treat above their head, at the level their nose would be when they sit pretty.

If they attempt to stand on their back legs to get the treat, you may be holding the treat too high, which will encourage them to stand up on their back legs to reach it. Go back to the first step and put them back into the "Sit" position, and again lift their paws while their backside remains on the floor.

The hand signal for "Sit Pretty" is a straight arm held over your dog's head with a closed fist. Place your Puggle beside a wall when first teaching this trick so that they can use the wall to help their balance.

A young Puggle puppy should be able to easily learn these basic tricks before they are six months old, and when you are patient and make your training sessions short and fun for your dog, they will be eager to learn more.

Excessive Jumping

Allowing any dog to jump is a serious mistake. It is one of the most undesirable of all traits in a companion canine. Many people are afraid of dogs, and find spontaneous jumping threatening. Since Puggles are prone to hip dysplasia and luxating patellas, excessive jumping could lead to a painful and expensive injury.

Don't assume that excessive jumping is an expression of friendliness. All too often it's a case of a dominant dog asserting his authority and saying, "I don't respect you." Dogs that know their proper place in the "pack" don't jump on more dominant dogs — or on more dominant humans! A jumper sees himself as the "top dog" in all situations.

Photo Credit: PuggleBaby.com and owner Rachael Remijn

As the dog's master, you must enforce the "no jumping" rule. Anything else will only confuse your pet. Dogs have a keen perception of space. Rather than retreating from a jumping dog, step sideways and forward, taking back your space that he is trying to claim.

You are not trying to knock your dog down, but he may careen into you and fall anyway. Remain casual and calm. Take slow, deliberate motions and protect the "bubble" around your body. Your dog won't be expecting this action from you, and he won't enjoy it. After several failed jumps, the dog will lose interest when his dominant message is no longer getting across.

Barking Behavior

Inside the house, Puggles will often vigorously defend their crate and the surrounding area from other pets. Extending their territoriality to the perimeter of the dwelling itself, Puggles will often bark at everything they see and hear, alerting you of the potential "threat."

This can make a Puggle a good watchdog, but it can also get you tossed out of an apartment complex or start an all-out neighbor war. Excessive barking creates serious problems when you live near other people. Normally a Puggle will bark a time or two in greeting and then stop, but if allowed to get in the habit of barking, the breed can be relentless.

To get to the bottom of problem barking, you must first try to figure out what is setting your dog off or, in the case of a Puggle, encouraging him. Is he lonely? Bored? Wanting attention? Overly excited? Anxious? Is he responding to something he's seeing, hearing, or smelling?

As with all problem behaviors, address barking with patience and consistency. If a firm "No" or "Quiet" fails to work, try spraying your dog with water from a mister or squirt gun. Aim for the face, but be careful not to get the water in the eyes. All you want to do is get your pet's attention and get him to stop barking.

For real problem barkers, humane bark collars can teach the dog through negative reinforcement. These collars release a harmless spray of citronella into the dog's nose in response to vibrations in the throat. The system, though somewhat expensive at $100/£60, works in almost all cases.

Chewing

Chewing is a natural behavior in dogs but can be excessive with Puggles, especially if the animal is expressing separation anxiety. If left undirected, a dog with a fetish for chewing is capable of causing unbelievable levels of destruction in your home.

Excessive chewing indicates some combination of anxiety or boredom, which may mean you need to get your dog out of the house more. Regardless, make sure your dog has proper chew toys, like Nylabones, that exist to be destroyed! If you catch your pet chewing on a forbidden object, reprimand him and take the item away. Immediately substitute an appropriate chew toy.

Digging

Digging, like other problem behaviors, is an expression of fear, anxiety, and/or boredom and something a Puggle can do with ruthless efficiency!

Digging is a difficult behavior to stop. An out-of-control digger can destroy your sofa or other piece of furniture. The best solution is to spend more time playing and exercising your pet. Also, consider enrolling your pet in a dog daycare facility so he will not be alone while you are at work and thus less susceptible to separation anxiety.

Begging

Begging behavior is definitely inherited from the Pug parent. Puggles are highly susceptible to weight gain, and they're quite good at using their charms to get whatever they want. Their faces are expressive and comical, and like a Pug, they know just when to cock their head to the side beguilingly.

Stay strong! Obesity can be life threatening. Make "people" food off limits from day one. If your pet becomes a serious beggar, confine him to another part of the house during meal times. If you can't ignore a set of pleading Puggle eyes imploring you to share your dinner, you're the real problem!

Chasing

Puggles, true to their inner Beagle, love to run, follow scents, and chase their quarry. It is essential that you keep your dog leashed during outings. A Puggle on a scent will not look left or right and can easily run into traffic in a busy urban area. Even if your dog does survive those kinds of perils, he won't come when you call and can get lost quickly. A Puggle moves like the very wind when he's running at top speed.

Biting

Any dog will bite if he is reacting out of pain or fear. Biting is a primary means of defense. Use socialization, obedience training, and stern corrections to control a puppy's playful nips.

Although Puggles typically grow out of it, they are ankle biters as puppies. Stern admonishment and a spritz of water in the face is generally all that's needed to curb the behavior.

If an adult Puggle displays biting behavior, it is imperative to understand the reasons for the biting. Have the dog evaluated for a health problem and work with a professional trainer.

Chapter 7 – Puggle Health

You are your Puggle's primary healthcare provider. You will know what is "normal" for your dog. Yours will be the best sense that something is "wrong," even when there is no obvious injury or illness. The more you understand preventive health care, the better you will care for your dog throughout his life.

Photo Credit: Lauren Goodman of Cottage Canines

Choosing Your Veterinarian

Working with a qualified veterinarian is critical to long-term and comprehensive healthcare. If you do not already have a vet, ask your breeder for a recommendation. If you purchased your pet outside your area, contact your local dog club and ask for referrals.

Make an appointment to tour the clinic and meet the vet. Be clear about the purpose of your visit and about your intent to pay the regular office fee. Don't expect to get a freebie interview and don't waste anyone's time! Go in with a set of prepared questions.

Be sure to cover the following points:

- How long has this practice been in operation?
- How many vets are on staff?
- Are any of your doctors specialists?
- If not, to which doctors do you refer patients?
- What are your regular business hours?
- Do you recommend a specific emergency clinic?
- Do you have emergency hours?
- What specific medical services do you offer?
- Do you offer grooming services?
- May I have an estimated schedule of fees?
- Do you currently treat any Pugs? Beagles? Puggles?

Pay attention to all aspects of your visit, including how the facilities appear and the demeanor of the staff. Things to look for:

- How the staff interacts with clients
- The degree of organization or lack thereof
- Indications of engagement with the clientele (office bulletin board, cards and photos displayed, etc.)
- Quality of all visible equipment
- Cleanliness and orderliness of the waiting area and back rooms
- Prominent display of doctors' credentials

These are only some suggestions. Go with your "gut." If the clinic and staff seems to "feel" right to you, trust your instincts. If not, no matter how well appointed the practice may appear to be, visit more clinics before making a decision.

Your Puggle's First Visit to the Vet

When you are comfortable with a vet practice, schedule a second visit to include your Puggle puppy. Bring all the dog's medical records. Be ready to discuss completing vaccinations and having the animal spayed or neutered.

Routine exam procedures include temperature and a check of heart and lung function with a stethoscope. The vet will weigh and measure the puppy. These baseline numbers will help chart growth and physical progress. If you have specific questions, prepare them in advance.

Vaccinations

A puppy's recommended vaccinations begin at 6-7 weeks of age. The first injection covers distemper, hepatitis, parvovirus, parainfluenza, and coronavirus.

Recommended boosters occur at 9, 12, and 16 weeks. In some geographical regions, a vaccine for Lyme disease starts at 16 weeks with a booster at 18 weeks.

The rabies vaccination is administered at 12-16 weeks and then generally every 3 years.

Evaluating for Worms

Puppies purchased from a breeder are almost always parasite free. Worms are more common in rescue dogs and strays. Roundworms appear as small white granules around the anus. Other types of worms can only be seen through a microscope. These tests are important since some parasites, like tapeworms, may be life threatening. Before a puppy's first visit, the vet will ask for a fecal sample for this purpose. If the puppy tests positive, the standard treatment is a deworming agent with a follow-up dose in 10 days.

It's best to take a stool sample at around 6-7 weeks to determine if the dog has worms or giardia. When the results are negative, it is not necessary to deworm them. Some breeders just give them deworming medicine routinely. It's very important a fecal sample be obtained and sent to a recognized lab for testing.

Spaying and Neutering

Breeder adoption agreements usually stipulate spaying and neutering before six months of age, but the procedures also carry health and behavioral benefits.

Neutering reduces the risk of prostatic disease or perianal tumors in male dogs. The surgery lessens aggressive behaviors, territorial instincts, urine marking, and inappropriate mounting.

Spayed females have a diminished risk for breast cancer and no prospect of uterine or ovarian cancer. There are no mood swings related to hormones or issues around the dog coming into season. It is a complete myth that dogs that have been neutered are more likely to put on weight.

"Normal" Health Issues

Although Puggles benefit from the principle of "hybrid vigor," all canines can face medical issues. The following are "normal" health-related matters that may need veterinary evaluation.

Pets that are inattentive or lethargic and that are not eating or drinking should be examined. None of these behaviors are normal for a Puggle.

Diarrhea

All puppies are subject to digestive upsets when they get into things they shouldn't, like human food or even the kitchen garbage. The resulting diarrhea should resolve within 24 hours.

During that time, the puppy should have only small portions of dry food and no treats. Give the dog lots of fresh, clean water to guard against dehydration. If the loose, watery stools are still present after 24 hours, take your Puggle to the vet.

The same period of watchful waiting applies for adult dogs. If episodic diarrhea becomes chronic, take a careful look at your pet's diet.

Photo Credit: Danielle Schnell of LuvAPuggle.com

Chances are good the dog is getting too much rich, fatty food and needs less fat and protein. Some dogs also do better eating small amounts of food several times a day rather than being offered 2-3 larger meals.

Allergy testing can identify the causes of some cases of diarrhea. Many dogs are allergic to chicken and turkey. A change in diet resolves their gastrointestinal upset immediately. Diets based on rabbit or duck are often used for dogs with such intolerances.

Either bacteria or a virus can cause diarrhea, which accompanies fever and vomiting. Parasites, in particular tapeworms and roundworms, may also be to blame.

Vomiting

Dietary changes or the puppy "getting into something" can also cause vomiting. Again, this should resolve within 24 hours. If the dog tries to vomit but can't bring anything up, vomits blood, or can't keep water down, take your pet to the vet immediately.

Dehydration from vomiting occurs faster than in a case of diarrhea and can be fatal. Your dog may need intravenous fluids.

When your dog is vomiting, always have a good look around to identify what, if anything, the dog may have chewed and swallowed. This can be a huge benefit in targeting appropriate treatment.

Other potential culprits include: hookworm, roundworm, pancreatitis, diabetes, thyroid disease, kidney disease, liver disease, or a physical blockage.

Bloat

Any dog can suffer from bloat. The condition is the second most common cause of death in dogs behind accidental trauma (like being struck by a car) in young dogs and cancer in elderly canines.

Some breeds are at higher risk than others are. Also known as gastric dilation/volvulus or GDV, bloat cannot be treated with an antibiotic or prevented with a vaccine. In roughly 50% of cases, bloat is fatal.

In severe cases, the stomach twists partially or completely. This causes circulation problems throughout the digestive system. Dogs that do not receive treatment go into cardiac arrest. Even if surgical intervention is attempted, there is no guarantee of success.

Signs of bloat are often mistaken for indications of excess gas. The dog may salivate and attempt to vomit, pace, and whine. Gas reduction products at this stage can be helpful. As the stomach swells, it places pressure on surrounding vital organs, and may burst.

All cases of bloat are a *serious* medical emergency.

Risk Factors

Larger dogs with deep chests and small waists face a greater risk of developing bloat. These include the Chow, Great Dane, Weimaraner, Saint Bernard, Irish Setter, and the Standard Poodle.

Eating habits also factor into the equation. Dogs that eat one large meal per day consisting of dry food are in a high-risk category as well. Feed three small meals throughout the day. This helps to prevent gulping, which leads to ingesting large amounts of air.

Experts recommend dry food for dogs, but don't let your Puggle drink lots of water after eating. Doing so causes the dry food in the stomach to expand, leading to discomfort and a dilution of the digestive juices.

Limit the amount of play and exercise after meals. A slow walk promotes digestion, but a vigorous romp can be dangerous.

Stress also contributes to bloat, especially in anxious or nervous dogs. Changes in routine, confrontations with other dogs, and moving to a new home can all trigger an attack.

Dogs between the ages of 4 and 7 are at an increased risk. Bloat occurs most often between 2 a.m. and 6 a.m., roughly 10 hours after the animal has had his dinner.

Prevention

Feed your pet small meals 2-3 times a day, limiting both water intake and exercise after eating. Take up your pet's water at mealtime and do not offer it to the dog for at least 30 minutes after your pet finishes his meal. Do not allow strenuous activity for at least an hour.

Test your Puggle's dry food by putting a serving in a bowl with water. Leave the material to expand overnight. If the degree of added bulk seems excessive, consider switching to a premium or organic food.

Keep an anti-gas medicine with simethicone on hand. (Consult with your veterinarian on correct dosage.) Consider adding a probiotic to your dog's food to reduce gas in the stomach and to improve digestive health.

If a dog experiences bloat once, his risk of a future episode is greater. Keep copies of his medical records at home, and know the location of the nearest emergency vet clinic.

Allergies

Like humans, dogs suffer from allergies. Food, airborne particles, and materials that touch the skin can all cause negative reactions.

Owners tend to notice a potential allergy when something changes in the dog's behavior to suggest discomfort like itching. Common allergy symptoms include chewing or biting of the tail, stomach, or hind legs, or licking of the paws.

In reaction to inhaled substances, the Puggle will sneeze, cough, or experience watery eyes. Ingested substances may lead to vomiting or diarrhea. Dogs can also suffer from rashes or a case of hives. Your poor Puggle can be just as miserable as you are during an allergy attack.

If the reaction occurs in the spring or fall, the likely culprit is seasonal pollen or, in the case of hot weather, fleas. Food additives like beef, corn, wheat, soybeans, and dairy products can all cause gastrointestinal upset.

As with any allergy, take away suspect items or try a special diet. Allergy testing offers a definitive diagnosis and pinpoints necessary environmental and dietary changes. The tests are expensive, costing $200+ / £120+.

The vet may recommend medication or bathing the dog in cool, soothing water. Special diets are also extremely helpful.

For acne-like chin rashes, switch to stainless steel, glass, or ceramic food dishes. Plastic feeding dishes cause this rash, which looks like blackheads surrounded by inflamed skin. Wash the dog's face in clear, cool water and ask the vet for an antibiotic cream to speed the healing process.

General Signs of Illness

Any of the following symptoms can point to a serious medical problem. Have your Puggle evaluated for any of these behaviors. Don't wait out of fear that you are just being an alarmist. Vets can resolve most medical problems in dogs if treatment starts at the first sign of illness.

Photo Credit: Mike & Tiffany Werner owners of Dexie & Morgan

Coughing and/or Wheezing

Occasional coughing is not a cause for concern, but if it goes on for more than a week, a vet visit is in order. A cough may indicate:

- Kennel cough
- Heartworm
- Cardiac disease
- Bacterial infections
- Parasites

- Tumors
- Allergies

The upper respiratory condition called "kennel cough" presents with a dry, hacking cough. It is a form of canine bronchitis caused by warm, overcrowded conditions with poor ventilation. In most cases, kennel cough resolves on its own.

Consult with your veterinarian. The doctor may prescribe a cough suppressant or suggest the use of a humidifier to soothe your pet's irritated airways.

When the cause of a cough is unclear, the vet will take a full medical history and order tests, including blood work and X-rays. Fluid may also be drawn from the lungs for analysis. Among other conditions, the doctor will be attempting to rule out heartworms.

A Note on Heartworms

Mosquitos spread heartworms (*Dirofilaria Immitis*) through their bites. They are thin, long parasites that infest the muscles of the heart, where they block blood vessels and cause bleeding. Their presence can lead to heart failure and death.

Coughing and fainting, as well as an intolerance to exercise, are all symptoms of heartworm. Discuss heartworm prevention with your vet and decide on the best course of action to keep your pet safe.

Other Warning Signs

- Excessive and unexplained drooling
- Excessive consumption of water and increased urination
- Changes in appetite leading to weight gain or loss

- Marked change in levels of activity
- Disinterest in favorite activities
- Stiffness and difficulty standing or climbing stairs
- Sleeping more than normal
- Shaking of the head
- Any sores, lumps, or growths
- Dry, red, or cloudy eyes

Often the signs of serious illness are subtle. Trust your instincts. If you think something is wrong, do not hesitate to consult with your vet.

Diabetes

Canines can suffer from three types of diabetes: *insipidus, diabetes mellitus*, and gestational diabetes. All point to malfunctioning endocrine glands and are often linked to poor diet. Larger dogs are in a higher risk category.

- In cases of *diabetes insipidus,* low levels of the hormone vasopressin create problems with the regulation of blood glucose, salt, and water.

- *Diabetes mellitus* is more common and dangerous. It is divided into Types I and II. The first develops in young dogs and may be referred to as "juvenile." Type II is more prevalent in adult and older dogs. All cases are treated with insulin.

- Gestational diabetes occurs in pregnant female dogs and requires the same treatment as diabetes mellitus. Obese dogs are at greater risk.

Abnormal insulin levels interfere with blood sugar levels. Any dog that is obese is at a higher risk for developing diabetes.

Symptoms of Canine Diabetes

All of the following behaviors are signs that a dog is suffering from canine diabetes:

- Excessive water consumption
- Excessive and frequent urination
- Lethargy / uncharacteristic laziness
- Weight gain or loss for no reason

It is possible your pet may display no symptoms whatsoever. Diabetes can be slow to develop, so the effects may not be immediately noticeable. Regular check-ups help to catch this disease, which can be fatal even when you do not realize that anything is wrong.

Managing Diabetes

As part of a diabetes management program, the vet will recommend diet changes, including special food. Your dog may need insulin injections. Although this may sound daunting, your vet will train you to administer the shots.

A dog with diabetes can live a full and normal life. Expect regular visits to the vet to check for heart and circulatory problems.

Hemorrhagic Gastroenteritis

Any dog can develop hemorrhagic gastroenteritis (HGE). The condition has a high mortality rate. Unfortunately, most dog owners have never heard of HGE. If a dog does not receive immediate treatment, the animal may well die.

Symptoms include:

- Profuse vomiting
- Depression
- Bloody diarrhea with a foul odor
- Severe low blood volume resulting in fatal shock within 24 hours

The exact cause of HGE is unknown, and it often occurs in otherwise healthy dogs. The average age of onset is 2-4 years. Approximately 15% of dogs that survive an attack will suffer a relapse. There is no definitive list of high-risk breeds.

The instant your Puggle vomits or passes blood, get your dog to the vet. Tests will rule out viral or bacterial infections, ulcers, parasites, cancer, and poisoning. X-rays and an electrocardiogram are also primary diagnostic tools for HGE.

Hospitalization and aggressive treatment are necessary. The dog will likely need IV fluids and even a blood transfusion. Both steroids and antibiotics prevent infection. If the dog survives, the animal should eat a bland diet for a week or more with only a gradual reintroduction of normal foods. In almost all cases, the dog will eat a special diet for life with the use of a probiotic.

The acute phases of HGE lasts 2-3 days. With quick and aggressive treatment, many dogs recover well. Delayed intervention for any reason means the outlook is not good.

Dental Care

Chewing is a dog's only means of maintaining his teeth. Many of our canine friends develop dental problems early in life because they don't get enough of this activity. Not all Puggles are prone to cavities. Most do suffer from accumulations of plaque and associated gum diseases. Often severe halitosis (bad breath) is the first sign that something is wrong.

With dental problems, gingivitis develops first and, if unaddressed, progresses to periodontitis. Warning signs of gum disease include:

- Reluctance to finish meals
- Extreme bad breath
- Swollen and bleeding gums
- Irregular gum line
- Plaque build-up
- Drooling, and/or loose teeth

The bacterial gum infection periodontitis causes inflammation, gum recession, and possible tooth loss. It requires treatment with antibiotics to prevent a spread of the infection to other parts of the body. Symptoms include:

- Pus at the gum line
- Loss of appetite
- Depression
- Irritability
- Pawing at the mouth
- Trouble chewing
- Loose or missing teeth
- Gastrointestinal upset

Treatment begins with a professional cleaning. This procedure may also involve root work, descaling, and even extractions.

With Proliferating Gum Disease, the gums overgrow the teeth causing inflammation and infection. Other symptoms include:

- Thickening and lengthening of the gums
- Bleeding
- Bad breath
- Drooling

- Loss of appetite

The vet will prescribe antibiotics and surgery is usually required.

Home Dental Care

There are many products available to help with home dental care for your Puggle. Some owners opt for water additives that break up tarter and plaque, but such products may cause stomach upset. Dental sprays and wipes are also an option, but so is gentle gum massage to help break up plaque and tarter.

Most owners incorporate some type of dental chew in their standard care practices. Greenies Dental Chews for Dogs are popular and well tolerated in a digestive sense. Another advantage is that dogs usually love them.

The treats come in different sizes and are priced in a range of $7 / £4.21 for 22 "Teeny Greenies" and $25 / £15 for 17 Large Greenies.

Brushing your pet's teeth is the ultimate defense for oral health. This involves the use of both a canine-specific toothbrush and toothpaste. Never use human toothpaste, which contains fluoride, toxic to your dog. Some dog toothbrushes resemble smaller versions of our own, but I like the models that just fit over your fingertip. I think they offer greater control and stability.

The real trick to brushing your Puggle's teeth is getting the dog comfortable with having your hands in his mouth. Start by just massaging the dog's face, and then progressing to the gums before using the toothbrush. In the beginning, you can even just smear the toothpaste on the teeth with your fingertip.

Try to schedule these brushing sessions for when the dog is a little tired, perhaps after a long walk. Don't apply pressure, which can stress the dog. Just move in small circular motions and stop when the Puggle has had enough of the whole business. If you don't feel you've done enough, stop. A second session is better than forcing your dog to do something he doesn't like and creating a negative association in his mind.

Even if you do practice a full home dental care routine, don't scrimp on annual oral exams in the vet's office. Exams not only help to keep the teeth and gums healthy, but also to check for the presence of possible cancerous growths.

Canine Eye Care

Check your Puggle's eyes on a regular schedule to avoid problems like clogged tear ducts. Also, many dogs suffer from excessive tearing, which can stain the fur around the eyes and down the muzzle.

As a part of good grooming, keep the corners of your pet's eyes and the muzzle free of mucus to prevent bacterial growth. If your dog is prone to mucus accumulation, ask your vet for sterile eyewash or gauze pads. Also consider having the dog tested for environmental allergies.

With longhaired animals, take the precaution of keeping the hair well trimmed around your pet's eyes. If you do not feel comfortable doing this chore yourself, discuss the problem with your groomer. Shorter hair prevents the transference of bacteria and avoids trauma from scrapes and scratches.

Puggles love to hang their heads out of car windows, but this can result in eye injuries and serious infection from blowing debris. If you don't want to deprive your dog of this simple pleasure, I recommend a product called Doggles. These protective goggles for dogs come in a range of colors and sizes for less than $20 / £12 per pair. The investment in protecting your dog's eyes is well worth it. All my pets have worn the Doggles without complaint.

Conjunctivitis

Conjunctivitis is the most common eye infection seen in dogs. It presents with redness around the eyes and a green or yellow discharge. Antibiotics will treat the infection. The dreaded "cone of shame" collar then prevents more injury from scratching during healing.

Cataracts

Aging dogs often develop cataracts, which is a clouding of the lens of the eye leading to blurred vision. The lesion can vary in size and will be visible as a blue-gray area. In most cases, the vet will watch, but not treat cataracts. The condition does not affect your pet's life in a severe way. Dogs adapt well to the senses they do have, so diminished vision is not as problematic as it would be for us.

Glaucoma

With glaucoma, increased pressure prevents proper drainage of fluid. Glaucoma may develop on its own or as a complication of a shifted cataract. Dogs with glaucoma experience partial or total loss of vision within one year of diagnosis.

Symptoms include swelling, excessive tearing, redness, and evident visual limitations. Suspected glaucoma requires immediate medical attention.

The Matter of Genetic Abnormalities

As a general rule of thumb, hybrid dogs tend to be healthier than either of their foundation breeds. The following conditions are already associated with the Puggle cross.

Hip and Elbow Dysplasia

Puggles are susceptible to hip dysplasia. This defect prevents the leg bones from fitting properly into the hip joint. It is a painful condition that causes limping in the hindquarters. The condition may be inherited or the consequence of injury and aging.

The standard treatment is anti-inflammatory medication. Some cases need surgery and even a full joint replacement. Surgical intervention for this defect carries a high success rate, allowing your dog to live a full and happy life.

Canine Arthritis

Dogs, like humans, can suffer from arthritis, which may develop in the presence of hip or elbow dysplasia as a secondary complication. Arthritis is a debilitating degeneration of the joints and is common in larger breeds.

As the cartilage in the joints breaks down, the action of bone rubbing on bone creates considerable pain. In turn, the animal's range of motion becomes restricted.

Standard treatments do not differ from those used for humans. Aspirin addresses pain and inflammation, while supplements like glucosamine work on improving joint health. Environmental aids, like steps and ramps, ease the strain on the affected joints and help pets stay active.

Arthritis also occurs as a natural consequence of aging. Management focuses on making your pet comfortable and facilitating ease of motion. Some dogs become so crippled that their humans buy mobility carts for them.

Photo Credit: Joerg Schubert owner of Parker

Luxating Patella

A dog with a luxating patella experiences frequent dislocations of the kneecap. The condition can affect one or both kneecaps. Surgery may be required to rectify the problem. Often owners have no idea anything is wrong with their dog's knee joint. Then the pet jumps off a bed or leaps to catch a toy, lands badly, and begins to limp and favor the leg.

The condition may be genetic in origin, so it is important to ask a breeder if the problem has surfaced in the line of dogs he cultivates. A luxating patella can also be the consequence of a physical injury, especially as a dog ages.

Any time you see your dog limping or seeming more fatigued than usual after exercise, have the dog checked out. Conditions like a luxating patella only get worse with time and wear, and need immediate treatment.

Hypothyroidism

Hyperthyroidism occurs when the thyroid gland fails to produce adequately. The deficiency of the hormone causes:

- Obesity
- Lack of energy
- Dulled mental abilities
- Infertility

The dog's hair may change, becoming brittle, dull, and falling out altogether while the skin gets dark and tough. The condition can be managed with daily medication that must be continued for life.

Stenotic Nares

Some Puggles are born with stenotic nares or pinched nostrils as a consequence of their short muzzles. The disorder makes it difficult for the dog to breathe properly, and thus the animal is exercise intolerant.

You can tell if a dog is not getting enough oxygen by looking at his gums, which will have a bluish tint. Mild cases of stenotic nares can be managed with weight control, limiting exercise during warm weather, and using a harness rather than a collar.

In severe cases, corrective surgery is needed to repair the abnormality.

Epilepsy

The brain disorder epilepsy can occur in Puggles for no
discernible reason, or it can be a result of genetic abnormalities.
The affected dog suffers seizures that can be controlled with
medication, but cannot be cured.

Idiopathic epilepsy occurs more frequently in male dogs and is
characterized by structural brain lesions. In the absence of
treatment, the seizures increase in severity and become more
frequent. With medication, however, the dog can live a full and
normal life.

Cherry Eye

The condition called "cherry eye" is an irritation of the third
eyelid. It appears as a bright pink protrusion in the corner of the
eye. Either injury or a bacterial infection causes cherry eye. It
may occur in one or both eyes and requires surgery to effect a
permanent cure.

Conditions Common to the Foundation Breeds

Any time you are considering a hybrid dog, it's important to get
a sense of health conditions specifically associated with each of
the foundation breeds.

Genetic Conditions in Pugs

In addition to hip and elbow dysplasia and luxating patellas,
Pugs are also known to have the following conditions.

Pug Dog Encephalitis

The cause of Pug Dog Encephalitis (PDE) is unknown, but the condition occurs most often in dogs that are closely related. Researchers believe it is a hereditary immune-mediated disease. The Pug's immune system attacks normal brain tissue causing:

- Changes in behavior
- Stiffness of the neck with head tilt
- Pressing of the head against objects and walls
- Seizures
- Poor coordination
- Walking in circles
- Confusion and disorientation
- Depression and lethargy
- Overall weakness
- Blindness

PDE can manifest as early as 6 months of age, but is seen most often in dogs aged 2 to 3 years. In many cases, PDE strikes quickly, progresses rapidly, and leads to sudden death, often during a seizure. In less severe cases, PDE can be controlled for a short period of time with anti-convulsant drugs. Unfortunately, PDE is always fatal. Contact your vet at the first sign of symptoms.

Brachycephalic Ocular Syndrome

Pugs, like all brachycephalic breeds, have large eyes that protrude. In dogs with excessively sagging lids that don't close completely, the corneas start to dry out.

The tear ducts can also become clogged and not drain properly, causing constant tearing and staining. The eyes often become scratched, sometimes due to injury or the presence of too many eyelashes, or those that are incorrectly placed.

The greatest potential for damage is to the cornea. Left untreated, even a minor scratch can progress to blindness as the eye begins to deposit the brown pigment melanin onto the cornea to make it tougher. Once in place, the melanin cannot be removed.

In Pugs with excessively bulging eyes, all of these problems come together to be described as a "syndrome." It may be necessary to administer lubricating eye drops and to maintain a constant vigil for potential injuries.

The eyes should be checked monthly to make sure there are no excess or oddly placed eyelashes. Monitor tear and mucus production and report anything to the vet that seems abnormal. Observe the cornea for any splotches that may be blue, white, or brown in color. Also watch the dog for squinting, which is a sign of pain.

Brachycephalic Obstructive Airway Syndrome

Brachycephalic obstructive airway syndrome is also called brachycephalic respiratory syndrome or congenital obstruct. Abnormalities in the upper airways make it harder for the dog to inhale, leading the dog to breathe through its mouth rather than the nose.

In mild cases, the dog will exhibit noisy breathing when at play and make snorting sounds when excited. Expect a lot of snoring. In severe cases, the animal will tire out quickly and may even faint or collapse from the exertion. The symptoms will be worse in humid, hot weather.

Primary symptoms include:

- Coughing
- Gagging

- Retching
- Vomiting

The most common secondary symptom is inflammation throughout the airways. Diagnosis typically occurs between 1 and 4 years of age. Males and females are affected equally. It is important to keep the dog's weight at a normal level.

Affected dogs should be kept in air-conditioned rooms. Limit their amount of exercise, and use a harness that does not place pressure on the neck. Do not use a regular collar under any circumstances.

Typical medications used include corticosteroids, non-steroidal anti-inflammatories, and even oxygen. These are management strategies only. It may be necessary to correct anatomical abnormalities surgically.

The earlier in the dog's life that surgery is performed, the better. Dogs under 2 years of age have the best prognosis in general terms, but your vet will have to give an individual prognosis based on the exact abnormalities present.

Portosystemic Shunt

The vascular anomaly called a portosystemic shunt diverts the flow of blood around the liver rather than into the organ. Consequently, the liver does not develop properly, and the blood is not filtered correctly.

The defect may be present at birth or develop later. The problem can be seen in any breed, but it is common in Pugs, Miniature Schnauzers, Cairn Terriers, Yorkshire Terriers, Scottish Terriers, Maltese, Golden Retrievers, Labrador Retrievers, Irish Wolfhounds, and Poodles.

Dogs with a portosystemic shunt develop poorly. The problem is often diagnosed when the dog is suffering from hepatic encephalopathy, which causes head pressing, swaying, an irregular gait, and seizures. The encephalopathy is caused by a buildup of toxins in the blood that then affect the brain.

Blood tests are used to diagnose the presence of a portosystemic shunt, which is then treated medically until the dog stabilizes, followed by surgery. The dog will then need a low protein diet until the blood normalizes.

Hemivertebrae

Brachycephalic breeds like the Pug often have a curled tail that may be a sign of a spinal abnormality called hemivertebrae. This is also seen in French and English Bulldogs and Boston Terriers.

If only the bones of the tail are affected, there is no major problem, but if the defect is in the back bone, the animal may suffer pain, be more susceptible to injury, and have an overly arched back.

Symptoms are evident by age 9 months when the spinal column is fully developed. Typically, two or more parts of the spinal column fail to fuse, causing compression. The dog's movement will be compromised, often to the point of paralysis.

Weakness tends to appear first in the hind limbs. The dog will show a reluctance to move or to stand. The gait will become uncoordinated, and the dog may have difficulty passing urine and voiding feces.

In mild cases, corticosteroid injections help to relieve inflammation, but severe instances require spinal surgery to correct the deformity. Pain management and restricted activity are a vital part of treatment.

The prognosis varies by individual, and clearly, treatment is extremely expensive.

Legg-Calve-Perthes Disease

Legg-Calve-Perthes Disease is a deformity of the ball of the hip joint. It is typically caused by some injury that prevents the head of the femur bone from receiving an adequate blood supply. Ultimately, the bone collapses and the cartilage becomes deformed. Inflammation and arthritis then cause pain and lameness.

Symptoms include chewing at the flank region, general irritability, and progressive lameness. The muscles of the limb will atrophy, and the dog will experience pain when the hip moves.

Surgery to remove the femoral head and neck is a highly effective treatment, although the dog may experience some residual lameness.

Entropion

Entropion is a condition in which the dog's eyelid turns inward, irritating the cornea. The issue becomes apparent in puppies with squinting and excessive tearing. In most cases, the condition resolves as the dog ages.

In severe instances, a canine ophthalmologist must tack the lids with stitches that will remain in place for a period of days or weeks until the correct "fit" is achieved. During healing, artificial tears are used to prevent drying of the eyes.

Distichiasis

A "distichia" is an eyelash that grows from an abnormal place on the eyelid or in an abnormal direction. This may occur on the upper or lower lid. Usually more than one is present; the plural is distichiae. This condition is similar to entropion.

If sufficiently severe, the abnormal eyelashes scratch the cornea causing ulceration. The eye and or conjunctiva may be red and inflamed.

Discharge can be present, and the animal may blink excessively, squint from pain, and keep the eye closed. If ulceration has developed, the affected cornea will appear to be bluish. Mild cases may require no treatment, or the simple use of lubricating drops. Severe cases must be addressed with corrective surgery, but in such instances, the prognosis is excellent.

Photo Credit: Jason & Jennifer Yates of Rainbowland Puggles

Genetic Conditions in Beagles

Of the conditions already discussed, Beagles are prone to hip dysplasia, seizure disorders like epilepsy, hypothyroidism, diabetes, cataracts, distichiasis, and allergies. Additionally, the occasional dwarf Beagle is born, and some dogs are congenitally deaf.

Because Beagles are highly active, they often suffer tears of the anterior cruciate ligament, which can require surgery. It is the canine equivalent of a human "blowing out" their knee.

Cardiac Disorders

Although rare, heart conditions seen in the breed include:

- Dilated cardiomyopathy (typically diagnosed when the dog develops a persistent cough and won't eat)
- Pulmonic stenosis (enlargement of the right side of the heart with an accompanying murmur)
- Ventricular septal defect (a hole in the heart)

All are managed with medication, but they significantly reduce the animal's projected lifespan.

Intervertebral Disk Disease

Like Dachshunds, Beagles often develop intervertebral disk disease (IVD). The condition presents with herniated disks in the lower back that cause severe pain that may radiate up to the neck.

Depending on the extent of the issue, surgery may be required, with some Beagles experiencing rear-quarter paralysis and the need for medical assistance carts to remain mobile.

Breeding Puggles

The decision to breed Puggles should only be undertaken for one reason — a desire to help cultivate the genetic quality of this emerging breed. For all but the most dedicated dog fanciers, this is not a viable proposition, because it requires an understanding of both Pug and Beagle genetics and access to breeding stock.

Breeding pedigreed dogs is not a get-rich quick scheme, nor is it an inexpensive hobby. Unfortunately, popular hybrids like the Puggle are attractive to people who are more interested in making money than in producing healthy, genetically sound dogs. Breeding dogs is a serious commitment to living creatures. Bottom line, if you don't know what you're doing, don't attempt to breed dogs of any sort.

The purpose of this book is not to educate potential breeders, but to introduce the Puggle to potential owners. You have a great deal to learn before you can even consider becoming a breeder, but if that is your ultimate goal — for all the right reasons — start making friends in the Puggle world now. Cultivating a mentor is an essential step toward owning and operating a successful, well-run breeding operation.

Chapter 8 - Dealing With an Older Puggle

What to Expect

Aging is a natural part of life for both humans and dogs. Sadly, dogs reach the end of their lives sooner than most humans do.

Once your Puggle reaches the age of 8 years or so, he can be considered a "senior" dog.

At this point, you may need to start feeding him a dog food specially formulated for older dogs, and you may need to take some other precautions as well.

In order to properly care for your Puggle as he ages, you might find it helpful to know what to expect. On this page, you will find a list of things to expect as your Puggle dog starts to get older:

• Your dog may be less active than he was in his youth – he will likely still enjoy walks, but he may not last as long as he once did, and he might take it at a slower pace.

• Your Puggle's joints may start to give him trouble – check for signs of swelling and stiffness, and consult your veterinarian with any problems.

• Your dog may sleep more than he once did – this is natural sign of aging, but it can also be a symptom of a health problem, so consult your vet if your dog's sleeping becomes excessive.

• Your dog may have a greater tendency to gain weight, so you will need to carefully monitor his diet to keep him from becoming obese in his old age.

• Your dog may have trouble walking or jumping, so keep an eye on your Puggle if he has difficulty jumping, or if he starts dragging his back feet.

• Your dog's vision may no longer be as sharp as it once was, so your Puggle may be predisposed to these problems.

• You may need to trim your Puggle's nails more frequently if he doesn't spend as much time outside as he once did when he was younger.

• Your dog may be more sensitive to extreme heat and cold, so make sure he has a comfortable place to lie down both inside and outside.

• Your dog will develop gray hair around the face and muzzle – this may be less noticeable in Puggles with a lighter coat.

While many of the signs mentioned above are natural side effects of aging, they can also be symptoms of serious health conditions.

If your dog develops any of these problems suddenly, consult your veterinarian immediately.

Care for an Older Puggle

When your Puggle gets older, he may require different care than he did when he was younger.

The more you know about what to expect as your Puggle ages, the better equipped you will be to provide him with the care he needs to remain healthy and mobile.

Here are some tips for caring for your Puggle dog as he ages:

• Schedule routine annual visits with your veterinarian to make sure your Puggle is in good condition.

• Consider switching to a dog food that is specially formulated for senior dogs – a food that is too high in calories may cause your dog to gain weight.

• Supplement your dog's diet with DHA and EPA fatty acids to help prevent joint stiffness and arthritis.

• Brush your Puggle's teeth regularly to prevent periodontal diseases, which are fairly common in older dogs.

• Continue to exercise your dog on a regular basis – he may not be able to move as quickly, but you still need to keep him active to maintain joint and muscle health.

- Provide your Puggle with soft bedding on which to sleep – the hard floor may aggravate his joints and worsen arthritis.

- Use ramps to get your dog into the car and onto the bed, if he is allowed, because he may no longer be able to jump.

- Consider putting down carpet or rugs on hard floors – slippery hardwood or tile flooring can be very problematic for arthritic dogs.

In addition to taking some of the precautions listed above in caring for your elderly Puggle, you may want to familiarize yourself with some of the health conditions your dog is likely to develop in his old age.

Elderly dogs are also likely to exhibit certain changes in behavior, including:

- Confusion or disorientation
- Increased irritability
- Decreased responsiveness to commands
- Increase in vocalization (barking, whining, etc.)
- Heightened reaction to sound
- Increased aggression or protectiveness
- Changes in sleep habits
- Increase in house soiling accidents

As he ages, these tendencies may increase – he may also become more protective of you around strangers.

As your Puggle gets older, you may find that he responds to your commands even less frequently than he used to.

The most important thing you can do for your senior dog is to schedule regular visits with your veterinarian. You should also, however, keep an eye out for signs of disease as your dog ages.

The following are common signs of disease in elderly dogs:

- Decreased appetite
- Increased thirst and urination
- Difficulty urinating/constipation
- Blood in the urine
- Difficulty breathing/coughing
- Vomiting or diarrhea
- Poor coat condition

If you notice your elderly Puggle exhibiting any of these symptoms, you would be wise to seek veterinary care for your dog as soon as possible.

Euthanasia

The hardest decision any pet owner makes is helping a suffering animal to pass easily and humanely. I have been in this position. Even though I know my beloved companions died peacefully and with no pain, my own anguish was considerable. Thankfully, I was in the care of and accepting the advice and counsel of exceptional veterinary professionals.

This is the crucial component in the decision to euthanize an animal. For your own peace of mind, you must know that you have the best medical advice possible. My vet was not only knowledgeable and patient, but she was kind and forthright. I valued those qualities and hope you are as blessed as I was in the same situation.

I am fortunate that I have never been forced to make this decision based on economic necessity. I once witnessed the joy of a biker who sold his beloved motorcycle to pay for cancer treatments for his German Shepherd. The dog meant more to him than the bike, and he burst into tears when the vet said, "We got it all."

But the bottom line is this. No one is in a position to judge you. No one. You must make the best decision that you can for your pet, and for yourself. So long as you are acting from a position of love, respect, and responsibility, whatever you do is "right."

Grieving a Lost Pet

Some humans have difficulty fully recognizing the terrible grief involved in losing a beloved canine friend.

There will be many who do not understand the close bond we humans can have with our Puggles, which is often unlike any we have with our human counterparts.

Your friends may give you pitying looks and try to cheer you up, but if they have never experienced the loss of such a special connection themselves, they may also secretly think you are making too much fuss over "just a dog."

For some of us humans, the loss of a beloved dog is so painful that we decide never to share our lives with another, because the thought of going through the pain of such a loss is unbearable.

Expect to feel terribly sad, tearful, and yes, depressed, because those who are close to their canine companions will feel their loss no less acutely than the loss of a human friend or life partner.

The grieving process can take some time to recover from, and some of us never totally recover.

After the loss of a family dog, first you need to take care of yourself by making certain that you remember to eat regular meals and get enough sleep, even though you will feel an almost eerie sense of loneliness.

Losing a beloved dog is a shock to the system that can also affect your concentration and your ability to find joy or be interested in participating in other activities that are a normal part of your daily life.

Other dogs, cats, and pets in the home will also be grieving the loss of a companion and may display this by acting depressed, being off their food, or showing little interest in play or games.

Therefore, you need to help guide your other pets through this grieving process by keeping them busy and interested, taking them for extra walks, and finding ways to spend more time with them.

Wait Long Enough

Many people do not wait long enough before attempting to replace a Puggle and will immediately go to the local shelter and rescue a deserving dog. While this may help to distract you from your grieving process, this is not really fair to the new furry member of your family.

Bringing a new pet into a home that is depressed and grieving the loss of a long-time canine member may create behavioral problems for the new dog that will be faced with learning all about their new home, while also dealing with the unstable energy of the grieving family.

A better scenario would be to allow yourself the time to properly grieve by waiting a minimum of one month to allow yourself and your family to feel happier and more stable before deciding upon sharing your home with another dog.

Managing Health Care Costs

Thanks to advances in veterinary science, our pets now receive viable and effective treatments. The estimated annual cost for a medium-sized dog, including health care, is $650 / £387. (This does not include emergency care, advanced procedures, or consultations with specialists.)

The growing interest in pet insurance to help defray these costs is understandable. You can buy a policy covering accidents, illness, and hereditary and chronic conditions for $25 / £16.25 per month. Benefit caps and deductibles vary by company.

To get rate quotes, investigate the following companies:

United States

http://www.24PetWatch.com
http://www.ASPCAPetInsurance.com
http://www.EmbracePetInsurance.com
http://www.PetsBest.com
http://www.PetInsurance.com

United Kingdom

http://www.Animalfriends.org.uk
http://www.Healthy-pets.co.uk
http://www.Petplan.co.uk

Afterword

Puggles are the third most popular hybrid dog in the United States for good reason. They are lighthearted, fun, healthy little creatures with adaptable dispositions and low exercise and maintenance requirements. They get along well with most other animals, but may chase cats, and they are a perfect dog for children.

Separation anxiety is an issue in this companion breed, so make certain you crate train your dog and are prepared to spend your off work hours in his company. This will, however, be a richly rewarding association for you, since Puggles are loyal and affectionate by nature.

Unlike many questionable hybrid pairings, mating a male Pug to a female Beagle produces an excellent medium-sized hybrid that tends to show the very best traits of both foundation breeds. This is the ultimate goal of such a cross and largely successful with Puggles.

With an emphasis on early training and a firm understanding of where Pug and Beagle traits complement or collide, the Puggle can be a perfect pet for singles or a growing family. And, as a bonus, they are long lived, with a maximum projected life expectancy of 15 years.

If you decide to welcome a Puggle into your life, be prepared for a fast-paced ride with an intelligent little dog who will take over your heart and your house pretty much from the moment he sets his paws inside your door!

Bonus Chapter 1 - Interview With Owner Carol VanHook

Carol, perhaps we could start by asking you how long you have been a Puggle owner and what made you choose a Puggle?

Our son during his 2005 high school junior year researched the rising star popular hybrid breed, the Puggle, convinced our family needed a new dog to replace a Pug we had and dearly loved – hoping this breed would handle heat changes and breathing issues better. After finding a litter of Puggle puppies for sale in the Des Moines Register, we headed out to Ottumwa, Iowa to check it out.

There were several adorable puppies. We picked this one because he was a real "chunk" and got stuck behind a table. We had to wiggle him out, and he seemed so appreciative. We have loved him ever since! He is almost ten! Our high schooler went off to college a thousand miles away; we still have our beloved Puggle!

How much did Smokey cost to buy and where did you buy him?

In 2005, the Puggle was beginning to be rising in popularity as a legitimate hybrid breed. We bought our chubby little fellow from a kennel in Ottumwa, Iowa. He cost $250 back then!

Do you have any advice to potential new buyers/owners?

Be prepared, Puggles are very active and strong as puppies. They need a lot of attention in the puppy stages as they chew and shred everything in sight.

Horror story: he got a hold of a computer cord and chewed it as a puppy. Fortunately, we were in the room with him and yanked him free. He was in shock but holding him tightly calmed him down. He had no injuries but this could have been fatal. PLEASE toddler proof the house for the puppy, just like you would for young children.

Magically after two years of puppyhood, they mellow and settle…as though the light switch turned on. Everyone familiar with Puggles told us, at three, our Puggle would calm down and they were right!

Has Smokey had any health issues?

Every August of his entire life, just like clockwork, Smokey gets a skin allergy all over his body. He requires a trip to the veterinarian for a round of cortisone pills, antihistamines, and an antibiotic if the skin breaks into "hot spots" and secondary bacterial infections.

Why do you think people should choose the Puggle over another breed of dog?

Puggles are very social and love people, children, and other pets. They love to please their owner. It is fun to take Puggles to a pet park and let them run. They will circle the park many times and come flying back to the owner, with their ears flopping in the wind. In the house, they also love to run circles, chase other pets, jump and flip for treats given to them, and will stand for an occasional squirt of whip cream!

They love their collar! Get a team sport or other personal collar, as they will wear it ever so proudly.

What would you say are common mistakes that you have seen Puggle owners make?

Table food! They much prefer table food over their healthy dog food mixes! This will put unwanted pounds on the Puggle. One thing is for certain, they love to eat! So spare the table scraps!

What are your feeding routines such as how often and what types of food do you feed Smokey?

The ten year old dog eats twice a day and gets ¾ a cup of dry food at each feeding. He loves to have an occasional blend of table food in his meal. This is not a good practice, and we are breaking him of the table food habit! He eats the grain-free dry mixes and gets an occasional wilderness trail treat, also 100% grain free.

Can you offer any grooming tips, advice and perhaps some accessories that you wouldn't be without?

The wire brush is handy in the spring as he begins to shed a winter coat. We sit outside and brush lots of hair away. He enjoys this grooming time.

Are there some tips and advice that you think most owners would be unaware of?

These dogs love to be walked. As a puppy, we would take Smokey in the car to our large fairgrounds and walk him upwards of three miles. He loved this time and began to think of the grounds as his own. Coming upon a strange item would shock him. I believe he could lead the way, on his own. He enjoyed meeting other people and animals along the way. Horses didn't faze him in the least!

As a much older dog, he loves a mile-long walk. He quickly learns a routine and seems to sniff his way, knowing where he has been before!

As an older dog, he has steps that allow him on our bed. He is happy to use these steps. He has a blanket on our bed. At bedtime, he watches us and quickly goes to his own spot. He loves to be wrapped up in this blanket for the night. A fan blowing on him seems to bother him. (As a puppy, we tried to train him to sleep in his own pet bed, but he only chewed up these beds!)

Are there any final thoughts that you feel the readers of this book would benefit from?

At about age seven, we began to take our little guy on long road trips. He settles in the back seat just fine. Hotels will charge extra but he is clean and well mannered. We take him to see our aging parents. He brings total joy to their lives and quickly adapts to being with them, each time we take him. He loves the new environment, as they have squirrels that scamper around an enclosed pool. He has only fallen in the pool twice and CAN swim! He is not fond of being in the pool, however! He does enjoy sunning around the pool and watching nature beyond the screened walls.

Have fun with your Puggle! In this day of digital photography, take lots of pictures. Start young, training your puppy to dress up: hats, capes, bowties, sweaters, etc. Go to the local dollar stores and pick up inexpensive costumes and props that can be easily adapted to dogs. Your pet will love the attention and learn to sit patiently for the photo shoot! Of course, they know they are the center of attention! Halloween, Christmas, St. Patty's Day, birthdays, etc. are fun times to make lasting photo memories!

Thank you Carol for providing this interview for our readers.

Bonus Chapter 2 - Interview With Doug Edmiston

In this extra interview, we find out a little bit more about Puggles from the perspective of a well-known breeder.

Can you tell us who you are and where you are based?

I am Doug Edmiston at Pugglesville and we are located in Vancouver, Washington USA.

What inspired you to become a breeder and did you start?

I was a Veterinarian's Assistant, and many times saw the disastrous results of poor breeding practices at our clinic as Puggles gained in popularity. We did start with Puggles; this is where we saw the biggest need. Amateur breeders were scrambling to churn out this very popular dog with no experience.

Is it possible to describe a fairly typical Puggle?

Aside from being fawn with black masks, the Puggle is the best of two great breeds of dog. They are playful, loyal little clowns with absolutely adorable personalities. They are active and charming and just adorably cute.

Do they attract a lot of interest and curiosity from the public?

Definitely. You can count on a walk that generally takes 15 minutes taking twice that long, or more.

Can you offer advice to people looking to buy a Puggle?

Research the breeder thoroughly, and get references. Anyone charging $500.00 or less for a Puggle is skimping somewhere in their breeding practices, and is likely a "pens and sheds in the backyard" type of breeder.

What types of people are buying Puggles and why?

All types of people are buying Puggles, but primarily people who want something different than the norm with the best character traits of both the Beagle and the Pug.

Are there things new owners do that perhaps frustrate you?

Take their new family member out and about before their vaccinations are completed.

The Puggle is not recognized by the American Kennel Club, is it a question or issue that is raised by many people?

People understand that Puggles are a hybrid. They also understand that cross-breeding results in hybrid vigor, and makes for a more hearty dog overall.

What challenges do you face in mating two different breeds?

It depends on the breeds and the size disparity, but Beagles and Pugs are highly compatible.

What type of health issues can a Puggle have?

Generally, cross-breeding obliterates all but the health issues both dogs have in common. Beagles and Pugs don't have many issues in common. I would say cherry eye is the only likely issue, and we've only seen two cases out of hundreds of Puggles.

What is the typical temperament of a Puggle?

Puppies can vary in temperament within a breed, and even within a litter. Generally though, Puggles are playful little clowns with absolutely adorable personalities.

Do you have any special feeding routines or diet?

Just a high quality food three times a day until they're six to eight months, then twice daily.

What colors and sizes are most popular?

Without a doubt, light fawn with the black mask.

As a breed expert, are there any tips you would like to share?

Just like with children, consistency is the key. Set boundaries for behavior, and BE CONSISTENT. Also, vaccinate regularly, and implement a parasite control regimen.

Doug Edmiston of Pugglesville
http://www.pugglesville.com/

Bonus Chapter 3 - Interview With Lauren Goodman

We find out about Puggles in Australia from a breeder who also works in a veterinary surgery.

Can you tell us who you are and where you are based?

I am a full time veterinary nurse, registered and licensed breeder and mother to furry, feathered and reptile kids – based in Sydney, NSW Australia. I work alongside other breeders, and enjoy spending each day with these animals. Always eager to learn more about animals, and meet and greet others.

How did you become a dog breeder?

I have always had a great interest in animals, and been incredibly passionate about my pets. As a kid, instead of reading children's novels – I would often read training books, breed books, and other informative chapters on animals. All puppies are cute, and all kids love puppies and animals – but this was something I never grew out of. When I graduated high school, I began working in the animal industry. Learning about animal husbandry, health, essential tools, behaviour and meeting other breeders and working closely, and relying on vets - was a great experience. I was keen to learn more, and become more involved.

From here I undertook Animal Studies, and started studying Veterinary Nursing – securing myself a full-time position in a local animal hospital. I want to learn as much as I can, and be as well informed as possible for looking after and breeding dogs. I was determined to do the right thing, ensuring I was to become an ethical breeder, striving to improve health and temperament. Becoming a Registered Breeder, and working in the vet clinic has been incredibly rewarding. Being so involved in the animal industry, and the lives of the puppies I find homes for is brilliant. I get to continue seeing these puppies as they grow, and as they visit the clinic for vaccinations, puppy preschool, desexing and so forth. Even in their new homes, I still feel for them as if they were my own.

Seeing how these puppies grow in their family homes, and as they come back to visit is ever so heartwarming. As these puppies mature and make their own families as happy, and bring as much joy and entertainment as my dogs do me – is the most rewarding part. The love they bring is unconditional.

How did you first come across Puggles?

Pugs had always been a favourite of mine, with their expressive faces, and fantastic personality – I got to see them all the time at the vet clinic, and adored getting to meet so many of these beautiful babies. There was an issue though, I got to see so many Pugs whilst working in the animal hospital, because there seemed to be so many issues that these dogs and their pet owners were struggling with health-wise.

I began looking into alternatives, and what would make a happy and healthy Pug-like family pet, without the problems? A friend of mine introduced me to the Puggle, and it was like love at first sight. The absolute epitome of a puppy; sweet, cuddly, playful and expressive puppy dog eyes, with chubby little bodies, and beautiful big ears! These puppies were not having difficulties breathing, and were as cute as a Pug, with the resilience of a Beagle.

Is there much awareness of the Puggle in Australia and do people recognize them in the street?

The Puggle is a fairly well-known dog where I am, in Sydney there are many dog parks, dog cafes and so on – where cross breeds seem to outnumber pure breeds at times. Australia's climate can be unforgiving, especially for short-muzzled bracycephallic type dogs. Pure Pugs are not an option for many families, who cannot cater to the necessary requirements that the squishy faced Pug demands. Puggles are a fantastic alternative, who can live both indoors and outdoors, enjoy trips to the beach, and weekend sports and family activities – yet are just as happy to lay on the lounge.

What types of people are buying Puggles and why?

Puggles are excellent pets, and are popular among families and young couples. The Puggle is an adaptable dog, that will enjoy city and suburban life – meeting and greeting people on the streets, visiting dog cafes, playing fetch in the park and running along the beach; the Puggle is a social butterfly who will enjoy all of the above, as much as they do coming home to the lounge in front of the TV. Country living is also suitable for a Puggle, who will enjoy running through paddocks, keeping an eye on chooks and sheep; and coming back up to lay on the porch on summer evenings, or in front of the fire on the cooler winter nights.

Is it possible to describe a fairly typical Puggle?

The typical Puggle is fawn or apricot in colour and has a black mask, with an evenly proportioned body – not as short, cobby and square set as the Pug, though not as long or heavy as the Beagle. Round, puppy dog eyes with dark eye rims, adorable floppy ears, the jaw can sometimes be slightly over shot – due to the Pug parentage. Nose should not be too pushed in. Most will have a tail that turns and falls over their back.

The Puggle is a friendly, affectionate dog that enjoys the company of its owner, and other dogs. A playful personality, and cuddle craving dog is fairly typical.

Can you offer advice to people looking to buy a Puggle?

Consider the best and worst of both breeds! The Puggle is an ideal family companion, but early training and socialisation is key (as with any dog). Do not over feed your Puggle! This is a common mistake many owners make. Give your puppy toys and the tools it needs to grow into a mature, and well-behaved dog. As a breeder and a vet nurse, we can offer the absolute best whilst the puppies in our care – but it is up to the new owner to continue. If one is not ready to commit the next 10 to 15 years with their Puggle, and provide them with the love and care they deserve, they should not bring one home. Vet care can be expensive, and puppies spend a lot of time visiting the vet clinic – especially in their first 12 months of owning them.

Are there things new owners do that perhaps frustrate you?

I have been the new owner of a puppy before, and can understand what it is like bringing home a new puppy and not knowing what to do. I feel for these owners, and do not see it as fair to become frustrated with them for not understanding something that, we wish they did. We offer extensive information, run through necessary care and guidelines with the puppies, and send them home with the things they will need to get started – and offer lifetime aftercare and advice for all our new families.

I am particularly fussy with the new families my puppies go to, and do my best to ensure they will be well looked after. Being particular with the families the puppies go to, and helping to answer questions, and provide advice prior to them taking the puppy home can avoid later frustration with new owners. Helping families to be as well informed as possible, there is less potential for frustration with these owners.

What sort of challenges do you face in mating two different breeds?

Sometimes you would be surprised! One of the hurdles considered, would be the size difference – but this is something we rarely have issues with (at the vet clinic, I have met and heard of surprising cross breeds – and accidental, yet natural matings occurring with 2 very different breeds, including: Dalmatian x Jack Russell and also Rottweiler x Maltese). One must consider temperament, and compatibility when it comes to mating, to ensure there are no disagreements with the dogs. There are some breeders with boys who can be quite rough at times, and in such circumstances artificial insemination is considered.

What is the typical temperament of a Puggle, so people know what to expect from their new pet?

Puggles are friendly and outgoing puppies, who will follow you around the house to everywhere you let them. Puggles enjoy family activities, and play time in the garden – but if allowed, will be more than content to curl up on the lounge and watch the television. Playful yet affectionate, provide toys to keep your puppy busy and attend puppy preschool, even if you're not a first-time dog owner. Easy-going pets, that are eager and willing to please.

Do you have any special feeding routines or diet?

A premium quality dry biscuit, recommended by your vet, is essential to ensure your dog has a well-balanced diet, and is given the nutrients they need. Dry biscuits will aid in keeping your dog's teeth clean, and if this is a premium dry food – will provide more nutrition than any home-cooked meals we can provide. Home-cooked food also encourages your dog to become fussy, and makes life a little difficult. Tinned food is not advised, as it has a high water content and often causes diarrhea. We offer fresh beef and cooked pasta, to lactating mothers and weaning puppies. Once 8 weeks of age and onwards, fresh beef is offered once or twice a week as a treat. Table scraps are a big no, and often lead to pancreatitis. Carrots are a family favourite, they are great for your dog's teeth and are an excellent boredom buster, they are cheaper than pigs' ears and not as high in fat!

It is important your puppy is getting the right amount of food and nutrition throughout the day, however it is important to remember NOT to overfeed your puppy – and don't leave a full bowl of food to sit there all day. Small frequent feeds are the key to success; we feed our puppies 3 to 4 meals a day (for smaller toy breeds it is essential that they are fed a minimum of 4 feeds a day as puppies. Smaller and more frequent feeds are required to maintain a healthy blood glucose level and avoid running into problems such as hypoglycemia.) Leaving a full bowl of food to sit there all day allows for the biscuits to go stale, and encourages your puppy to become a fussy eater, which is something you definitely want to avoid. Make sure fresh, clean water is always available and easily accessible for your puppy or dog at all times.

Our adults are fed once a day, as part of our morning routine – we then go on to feed the birds, feed the cats and the turtles – then sit by the koi pond and have our own morning coffee.

Below are things to be aware of, some of what you can and cannot feed your dog – be mindful and always check with your vet if there is something you're not too sure about.

Do

Do feel free to offer some of those listed below, as a healthy treat or as part of a balanced diet:

- Lean Meats
- Salmon
- Sardines

- Large Raw Bones (no chicken wings or bones which could easily splinter. It's ok for dogs to chew on larger bones, then remove once the meat is off the bone. Eating the bone can cause constipation, and also chip your dog's teeth)
- Fruits such as apples, oranges, bananas, watermelon (avoid seeds)
- Veggies including carrots, green beans, cucumber, zucchini, cooked pumpkin or sweet potato – my dogs love fresh, raw carrots!
- Cooked white rice or pasta
- Peanut butter – a yummy treat, great for KONGS
- Chicken/soup stock – great to make frozen treats for a hot day!

Don't

Don't offer your dog any of the things listed below, if you have concerns please contact your vet immediately:

- Avocado
- Onions (and garlic)
- Caffeine
- Grapes and raisins
- Milk
- Macadamia nuts
- Chocolate and lollies
- Fat trimmings – can cause pancreatitis
- Cooked bones of any sort may splinter and cause choking
- Small raw bones – constipation, requiring an enema under anaesthetic
- Persimmons, peaches, plums
- Moldy foods – no good for you or your dog

What colors and sizes are most popular?

Apricot and red Puggles are a definite favourite, with fawns being another. Blacks are popular but not common, and other less frequently seen colours include tricolour, black and white, lemon and white, liver and white, silver. Sizes are fairly standard, and rarely as small as the Pug or as large as the Beagle.

As a breed expert, are there any 'essential' tips you would like to share with new owners?

Making sure you can provide your puppy with all that it will need through the many years of its life is very important. In the first year alone, you have vaccinations, microchipping, desexing, parasite prevention, puppy preschool, toilet training, socialisation – just to name a few! Consistency is key in regards to training. Make sure your Puggle knows to come back and is well behaved, and have spent time training your dog before letting them off lead at the park. Stick to fenced-in areas. More importantly, love and enjoy your Puggle – and all the years of entertainment and companionship they have to bring you.

What health issues do Puggles tend to suffer from?

Puggles are a generally hardy and healthy dog, being that the Puggle is not a pure bred or a pedigree – but in fact a cross between the Pug and the Beagle – they tend to inherit hybrid vigour. This wider gene pool allows for more genetic diversity and less chance of congenital diseases and disorders.

In saying so – the Puggle is not entirely problem free, and there are things to look out for. General health concerns for the Puggle do relate more to their physical form however. Listed below are details:

Obesity: look out! Both the Pug and the Beagle are quite ravenous at the dinner table, and will always seem to be wanting more – do not give in! An over-fed Puggle, will quickly become over weight. Obesity can contribute to a number of problems, including putting added and unnecessary weight and pressure on the joints, which is a concern for arthritis.

Ear infections: those oh so cute, and big floppy ears!! As with any breed whose ears do not stand erect, the risk of ear infections is high. Though more common in the warmer weather, these ear infections can occur all year round. This can be painful, and quite irritating, and needs veterinary attention. A vet will need to take a swab of the dark coloured wax from your dogs ears, smear the sample on a glass slide, and analyse by using a microscope to determine the type of infection present. This normally requires two weeks' worth of medicated ear drops, and rechecks by the vet to ensure the infection has cleared.

Ways you can help avoid ear infections in your Puggle include making sure under their ears are nice and dry (especially after a bath, swimming, or playing in the water) as the moist hair becomes trapped under the ear, creating a warm breeding ground for bacteria leading to ear infections. Checking your dog's ears every couple weeks to make sure they are nice and clean, is also important.

Dental disease: small breed dogs are renowned for having bad dental health, with plaque and gingivitis forming and causing pain and discomfort. A well-balanced diet, including a premium quality dry biscuit, is vital for a good start. These dry biscuits will help to keep your dog's teeth in better condition than any wet or home-cooked meals. Treats are ok in moderation, but imagine if humans were to eat spam or similar consistency food all our lives – and never brush our teeth? Pretty rotten, right? In addition to dry biscuits, offering dental sticks and treats formulated for dogs can help, as can dental toys.

Brushing your dog's teeth is also possible, and also recommended. You must use dog toothpaste though, and not human toothpaste. There are different doggie toothbrushes and finger brushes available, but you can also use a soft child's toothbrush. Brushing your dog's teeth will help to avoid plaque buildup and gum recession.

Some dogs who have not had assistance from their owners to take care of their teeth, may require their teeth to be cleaned (scale and polish, under anaesthetic). Some of these will require tooth extractions if the tooth or tooth root is rotting and decayed, as a result of bad dental health.

One should treat their dog's teeth, as they would their own.

Stenotic nares: though not common in the Puggle, possible with Pugs and some Pug crosses is the stenotic nares – this is when the nostrils seem pinched in – more severely in some cases than others. Some of these nostrils will grow with the dog in the first few months of life, but many will require a stitch to be put in to widen the nostril (this is normally done at 6 months of age, time of desexing).

Cherry eye: Again not common in Puggles, though does tend to occur more frequently in bracycephalic typed dogs – cherry eye is when the third eyelid protrudes or pops out, appearing red and swollen. This requires medicated eye ointment, to help keep the eye lubricated, and often contains a steroid as well. These eye medications are first trialled, and in some cases the cherry eye is corrected within a matter of a couple of weeks. For those which don't correct within this time, surgery is required.

Luxating Patellas: not incredibly common in Puggles, though generally common with smaller breed dogs – this is when a dog has slipping/sliding kneecaps. This can often be determined in puppies, and there are various grades. Some which are less severe may self correct as the puppy grows, others will worsen and require corrective surgery. Breeding from parents with luxating patellas should never be done – this does predispose their puppies to have the same issue, though healthy parents can still sometimes produce offspring with luxating patellas. Luxating patellas can be detected in puppies as young as 6-8 weeks of age.

Heat stroke: ensure your Puggle always has fresh, cool water and shade available.

These are some of the main things to look out for, that I have found relative to the breed. Ensuring your puppy has been health checked by a certified veterinarian, and giving your puppy/dog the best tools and care you can to look after them, will contribute immensely to their health and wellbeing.

Lauren Goodman of Cottage Canines
http://www.cottagecanines.com/

Glossary

Abdomen – The surface area of a dog's body lying between the chest and the hindquarters; also referred to as the belly.

Allergy – An abnormally sensitive reaction to substances including pollens, foods, or microorganisms. May be present in humans or animals with similar symptoms including, but not limited to, sneezing, itching, and skin rashes.

Anal Glands – Glands located on either side of a dog's anus used to mark territory. May become blocked and require treatment by a veterinarian.

Arm – On a dog, the region between the shoulder and the elbow is referred to as the arm or the upper arm.

Artificial Insemination – The process by which semen is artificially introduced into the reproductive tract of a female dog for the purposes of a planned pregnancy.

Back – That portion of a dog's body that extends from the withers (or shoulder) to the croup (approximately the area where the back flows into the tail).

Backyard Breeder – Any person engaged in the casual breeding of purebred dogs with no regard to genetic quality or consideration of the breed standard is referred to as a backyard breeder.

Bitch – The appropriate term for a female dog.

Blooded – An accepted reference to a pedigreed dog.

Breed – A line or race of dogs selected and cultivated by man from a common gene pool to achieve and maintain a characteristic appearance and function.

Breed Standard – A written "picture" of a perfect specimen of a given breed in terms of appearance, movement, and behavior as formulated by a parent organization, for example, the American Kennel Club or in Great Britain, The Kennel Club.

Brows – The contours of the frontal bone that form ridges above a dog's eyes.

Buttocks – The hips or rump of a dog.

Castrate – The process of removing a male dog's testicles.

Chest – That portion of a dog's trunk or body encased by the ribs.

Coat – The hair covering a dog. Most breeds have both an outer coat and an undercoat.

Come Into Season – The point at which a female dog becomes fertile for purposes of mating.

Congenital – Any quality, particularly an abnormality, present at birth.

Crate – Any portable container used to house a dog for transport or provided to a dog in the home as a "den."

Crossbred – Dogs are said to be crossbred when each of their parents is of a different breed.

Dam – A term for the female parent.

Dew Claw – The dew claw is an extra claw on the inside of the leg. It is a rudimentary fifth toe.

Euthanize – The act of relieving the suffering of a terminally ill animal by inducing a humane death, typically with an overdose of anesthesia.

Fancier – Any person with an exceptional interest in purebred dogs and the shows where they are exhibited.

Groom – To make a dog's coat neat by brushing, combing, or trimming.

Harness – A cloth or leather strap shaped to fit the shoulders and chest of a dog with a ring at the top for attaching a lead. An alternative to using a collar.

Haunch Bones – Terminology for the hip bones of a dog.

Haw – The membrane inside the corner of a dog's eye known as the third eyelid.

Head – The cranium and muzzle of a dog.

Hip Dysplasia – A condition in dogs due to a malformation of the hip resulting in painful and limited movement of varying degrees.

Hindquarters – The back portion of a dog's body, including the pelvis, thighs, hocks, and paws.

Hock – Bones on the hind leg of a dog that form the joint between the second thigh and the metatarsus. Known as the dog's true heel.

Inbreeding – When two dogs of the same breed that are closely related mate.

Lead – Any strap, cord, or chain used to restrain or lead a dog. Typically attached to a collar or harness. Also called a leash.

Litter – The puppy or puppies from a single birth or "whelping."

Muzzle – That portion of a dog's head lying in front of the eyes and consisting of the nasal bone, nostrils, and jaws.

Neuter – To castrate or spay a dog thus rendering them incapable of reproducing.

Pedigree – The written record of a pedigreed dog's genealogy. Should extend to three or more generations.

Puppy – Any dog of less than 12 months of age.

Separation Anxiety – The anxiety and stressed suffered by a dog left alone for any period of time.

Sire – The accepted term for the male parent.

Spay – The surgery to remove a female dog's ovaries to prevent conception.

Whelping – Term for the act of giving birth to puppies.

Withers – The highest point of a dog's shoulders.

Wrinkle – Any folding and loose skin on the forehead and foreface of a dog.

Index

Lightning Source UK Ltd.
Milton Keynes UK
UKOW01f1629010218

317218UK00005B/467/P